THE CARAVAN TO NOWHERE

PETER KENDALL

© Peter Kendall 2010

Published by Peter Kendall, Kemsing, Kent TN15 6TE

Typesetting and layout by James Morton-Robertson

The right of Peter Kendall to be identified as the Author of the Work has been asserted by him in accordance with the Copyright, Designs and Patents Act 1988.

All rights reserved. No part of this publication may be reproduced, stored in a retrieval system, or transmitted, in any form or by any means without the prior permission of the Author, nor be otherwise circulated in any form of binding or cover other then that in which it is published and without a similar condition being imposed on any subsequent purchaser or owner of this published Work.

ISBN13   978-0-9564715-1-2

NOTES

For the reader who wishes to keep track of the names of the various characters, the chronology of events, and the geography of the Valhalla Haven, a series of appendices, including a map, have been attached to the end of the text.

The measurement of the passing of time, in the Valhalla Haven, was very similar to that used today on Planet Earth. A year (one crop growing cycle) was split into fifty-two, seven-day weeks (resulting in a 364 day year). The length of a Valhalla Haven year being not so different in length to a year on Planet Earth.

Front cover – NASA image of The Magellanic Cloud
Image facing Chapter 1 - Valhalla Haven. Painting by Al Hart FRSA

To my daughters Sian, Clare and Katharine

to whom the story was originally told.

Epigraph

Children's 'elimination' chant

Traveller, Traveller, I know you

Our five fields are still in view

Beacon, Beacon, guide us true

Silent partner, out goes you.

Anon

Origin – Hope District   Date – The Twilight Years

PROLOGUE

First voice	"Please, tell us a story."
Second voice	"All right, but what sort of story?"
First voice	"Tell us one that happened in our distant past. They're always the most interesting."
Second voice	"Well, perhaps I should tell you one about a particular rocky planet."
First voice	"And what exactly is a rocky planet?"
Second voice	"You know, one of those small solid and round masses of material that are often found orbiting near the younger stars."
First voice	"I remember now, but that sort of planet doesn't sound very interesting."
Second voice	"They can be, when they have Life on them as this one did, which was actually living on its surface."
First voice	"Human life like ours?"
Second voice	"No, it was an earlier form of ourselves."
First voice	"What does that mean?"
Second voice"	Well, if you'd stop asking questions, I could get on with the story, and put everything in the proper order. What I am about to tell you happened a very long time ago. It took place in that Galaxy we can see in the sky; the one we all originally came from. The rocky planet was first called Paradise, and it played an indirect part in our own history."
First voice	"How did these humans come to be on Paradise in the first place?"
Second voice	"That's what the first part of my story explains. Do you want to hear it?"
First voice	"Does it contain adventure, mystery, romance, and tragedy?"
Second voice	"Yes, plenty of all four. If you're sure that you're comfortable, I'll tell you how it all came about."

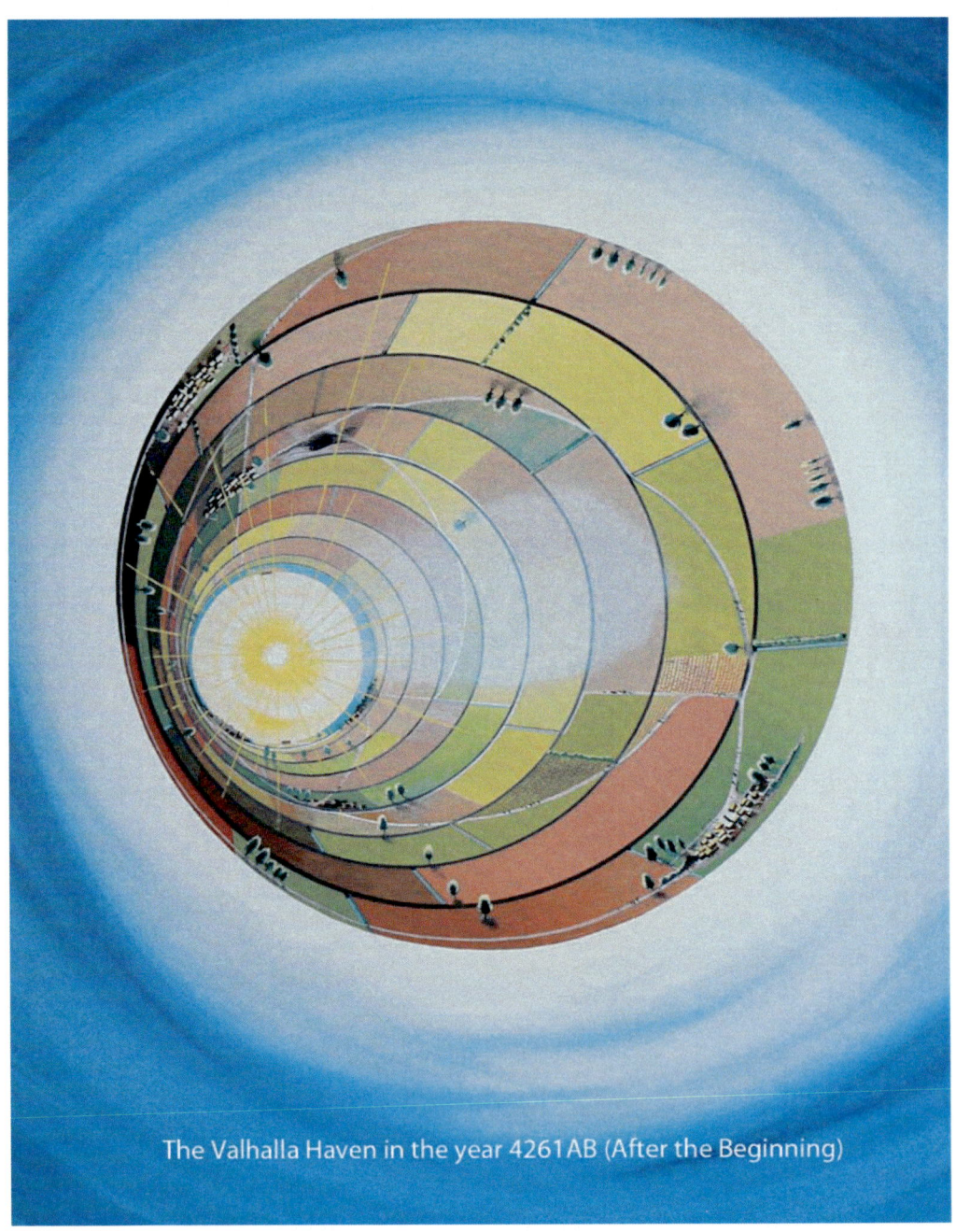

The Valhalla Haven in the year 4261AB (After the Beginning)

Chapter One – The Valhalla Haven

When the sand clock, which hung in the village hall tower, was nearly empty Javan knew that it was time for him to be on the move. He put the finishing touches to a drainage channel he was clearing in a corn field near the village. Then with his thick muscular arms he hefted the spade to a spot where it would be safe but not forgotten, and used his wiry legs to climb quickly up onto the raised path nearby.

He strode between the mud and brick houses on the outskirts of Hope village, then its bustling main street and beyond. He arrived shortly after at the foot of the Great Stairs about a quarter of an hour before noon. By looking back from even the lowest step of the stairs, on a clear day, he could see practically every field, homestead and village there was to see in the World. For him, the view was as if he were standing at the bottom of a long straight circular-shaped valley. The sides of the valley, however, instead of rising to hill tops continued to curve upwards until they were vertical. Then, even more strangely, the fields and paths continued to curve inwards until they met high overhead. People walking overhead amongst the green and brown 'patchwork' of the fields appeared to be upside down and like ants crawling across a ceiling. Javan could also see, by a mere twist of his head, each End of the World. These were flat, made of some seemingly indestructible material, vertical and almost featureless, with the exception of two stone stairs, diametrically opposite each other on one End; and the sun positioned at the exact centre of the other End. This scene wasn't regarded by the Bell-ringer as odd because it was all that he had ever known.

Hope village was situated at the foot of one of the Ends of the World; the end, known as Bell End. One of the stairs on its face began almost within the village and climbed sideways, in a slowly rising concave shape, two and half strides wide. The Stairs ended in a small platform high above ground level, less than a quarter of the way up the End of the World.

Glancing, with a smile, at two sandal-footed young school girls sitting forlornly on the lower steps of the Stairs, Javan began his second of four daily journeys to the platform at the top. He wore a light pig-skin jacket and matching trousers, and climbed cautiously, steadily and silently, conserving his breath as far as he was able, and avoiding the precipice on his right. Soon the thatched roof tops of Hope Village were left below and behind. The heat of the sun, shining from the far end of world, was reflected off the wall on his left, wringing perspiration from his face. About half way to the top Javan came across two boys sitting with their backs to the wall, fear in their eyes at the sheer drop to the fields below. Grinning, he grunted a sympathetic greeting as he passed, remembering his own fear the first time his father had brought him up the Stairs many years before.

As he neared the platform at the top of the stairs, he slowed, not through fatigue but because the Mother World didn't grip him quite so tightly here, and it wouldn't do to over-balance. There before him, sitting on the very top step, was the robed Priest (and teacher) Zepho, and three pupils in tunics, white-faced but triumphant, as they tried to concentrate on various aspects of the vista in front of them. The Bell-ringer circumvented the school party, and stepped onto the platform. Breathing deeply, he took a bone club that lay nearby and prepared to strike the giant bell that hung sideways, on the End of the World above the platform. The Bell, called Hemlock was about as tall as the bell-ringer and three hand spans thick. The only features on its dull surface were a number of star shaped markings running in an arc from the Bell's exact centre.

Taking care not to go too close to the unfenced edge of the platform, the Bell-ringer balanced himself, and swung the club against the Bell. There rang out over the fields and hamlets, down the great tunnel shape of the World to the lake at the far end, the peals of the great Bell Hemlock. He struck Hemlock four times, being noon, when the sun was at its brightest, whilst his shadow emulated his movements on the end of the world. Above, below and on either side, out in the fields, the farm people relaxed for the midday rest period; dogs barked and babies woke. All over the World men were resetting their sand clocks for the second half of the day. At the other end of the World, School End, after a count of twelve, the chimes of the Bell were heard as a distant roll of sound. Classes were dismissed for the day, the Priests settled to their studies and the hamlet markets began to pack up and disperse.

With his chest still heaving, Javan shaded his eyes from the sun which hung in the distance and proud of the circular face of School End. Already a thick haze was forming in the central axis of the World that would turn into the usual afternoon rainstorm. Soon the stairs would become wet and slippery; he would have to be quick to avoid this. Near the Bell, up against the end of the World were two piles of stones. As Javan moved a stone from one pile to the other, he spoke to Zepho.

"There's two of your boys sitting half-way up" he said; "And the girls have stayed at the bottom" he went on, "I don't know why you persist in trying to get them up here"

Zepho stopped trying to point out the relative positions of the hamlets, Harp and Happen overhead. "To stretch their minds a little, Bell-ringer" he said "and to give them perspective. It's difficult to grasp the World as a whole from any point at ground level. From up here you can see how the ridges between the fields form hoops in a giant barrel, and the way that the villages are so spread out on the inside of the barrel that, no matter where you are, there is always at least one above you. And besides", he added, indicating the Bell, "Old Hemlock here is more important that you think."

"Of course she's important" said Javan stiffly. "Where would we all be without her." He didn't particularly like being treated by Zepho as if he were one of his pupils. Javan was very proud of his job which he thought to be very important.

Where indeed, thought Zepho to himself grimly and it wouldn't just be a matter of not knowing the time of day. Out loud he said "Look above and below the Bell, boys, do you see the lettering there? Take a good look because it doesn't appear anywhere else, except around the Bell Molock at the top of the other set of stairs above us. Perhaps the Bell-ringer will tell us what the lettering says. Will you Bell-ringer?" Javan glanced sharply at the Priest, unsure as to whether Zepho was trying to trick him or not. Of course he knew what the lettering said, but only because he knew it by heart. Only the Priests could actually have read it.

The letters were large, and made of the same material as the end of the world in which they were set. Though partly obscured by the Bell, Javan quoted from memory.

"Valhalla Haven, is what it says above the Bell" he said. "And, 'Hemlock' below. Now, perhaps Father Zepho can tell us what it means."

Zepho was silent for a moment, then blew his nose on a piece of rag whilst deciding how to phrase his reply. "The legends say that the words above the Bell are magic letters placed there to prevent evil spirits, which sometimes enter the world on the wings of the Bell chimes, from doing the human race any lasting harm. It is clear they have, so far, been reasonably effective and must have been placed there at the Beginning. I like to think of them as a kind of Blessing." The Priest fell silent and, for a few moments, each member of the party was absorbed in his own thoughts.

The Bell-ringer made ready to leave the platform. He had now recovered his breath but was anxious to leave last in case any of the boys should be tempted to re-arrange the 'day' stones. He waited for Zepho to guide his boys down ahead of him. However, one of the taller and older boys still had a final question and neither the Bell-ringer nor the Priest knew of any answer to it.

"Why are there ten star shaped markings on the Bell?" asked Adam.

In a potato field half the world away, near Happen Hamlet, a pretty dark-haired girl straightened her back as the bell chimes of Hemlock rolled out announcing noon and the midday rest period. She looked up as if to catch a glimpse of her boyfriend who, as far as she knew was in school but, at that very moment, was asking difficult questions of the Bell-ringer. Physically the girl took after her mother, with quick, responsive manner and a fondness for chattering. She had also inherited her father's brain and sense of humour, but not his love of farming. The girl was fourteen at this time, having first met Adam a short time before at the annual March around the World on the Halfway Path. She had thought him very good looking and funny but, after the hour and a half it took to walk all the way round the World, also decided she liked his confidence. This latter quality made him appear much older than he actually was. Adam, if asked, would probably have said he was attracted to her figure, unless it was the girl doing the asking. In that case he would have said her smile, or her cheerfulness. It soon became clear to both of them that they shared a common interest, to find out everything they could about the world about them.

At the sound of the Bell, the girl quietly laid aside the hoe she was using, and made off as fast as she could to Happen Hamlet, a short distance up the track. Her short, rather muddy, pig skin skirt somewhat limited the length of stride she could take but her scruffy sleeveless jacket was carefully buttoned up so as not to flap. She ignored the shouts and whistles from the boys in the fields along the way and, dodging the midge swarms and a particularly large bees nest, made her way to one of the huts amongst a cluster of mud brick, thatched houses where the Scribe, Gether, lived. The Hamlet streets were narrow, for space was precious and children chanted, played, and fought in available open spaces. In her hand the girl clutched some vegetables which she hoped to trade for the scribe's service, not having enough wooden coins.

Inside Gether's house, there were several people sitting on the floor waiting for his attention. The only sounds were of scuffling feet and the scratch of Gether's quill. The house was sparsely fitted out with a bare minimum of furniture, the only light coming in through an open window, and dust lying on every surface. Gether was a bachelor in his fifties, and not very good at housekeeping.

"You again, young lady" said Gether looking up from his writing. "A runner has just passed through to Happy Village, nothing more will go until tomorrow sundim."

The girl said nothing, but sat down anxiously to await her turn with the Scribe. Several of those present, and also waiting, were friends of the family. News would rapidly get back to her parents if there was anything unusual about her message.

The girl was quite used to the fact that it was very difficult to go anywhere in the world without meeting relatives, and practically impossible to avoid seeing friends. The official lists of the World population kept at the Hall of Silence had about five hundred and fifty names, and this meant that nearly everyone was known to everyone else by sight, if not by name.

When her turn came, the girl had her message ready. It was a cleverly constructed and mild enough greeting to Adam containing within it a secret date and location for their next assignation. Gether wrote the message out carefully and then handed her the parchment in exchange for the proffered new potatoes. Just as she was leaving Gether's hut, the girl had the misfortune to bump into a boy called Shepho, who was big for his age, and had a longstanding reputation as a village bully. Shepho grabbed hold of her arm and a grin appeared on his freckled face.

"Out of my way, Shepho" demanded the girl wearily.

"Just a moment, little girl, you seem to be in an awful hurry." He noticed the parchment and made a grab for it. "A message to your boyfriend?" he continued teasingly.

The girl managed to keep it out of his clutches for a while. Whilst they struggled, she gasped "Please Shepho, let me go. I'll get into terrible trouble if I'm not home soon."

Shepho continued to try and get hold of the parchment, shifting his grip on the girl's arm. "Not until I see what you've written" he said spitefully, "or you give me a kiss. Which is it to be. Hurry up and decide, or I may demand both!" Several onlookers obviously disapproved of Shepho's aggressive behaviour but none of them seemed inclined to interfere, on the girl's behalf, against so strong a boy.

The girl took a quick decision. At one and the same time she thrust the parchment into Shepho's face and, as his attention was diverted to protecting his eyes, twisted free of his grip. The girl staggered back, free, but without the parchment. Keeping well away from Shepho, she swore and spat at him. The girl then fled the hamlet, rubbing her arm where an angry red mark was now appearing, and ran all the way home to 'Welcome' farm.

In the meantime, over near Hope Village, Father Zepho had descended from the platform and was marshalling the school party at the foot of the Stairs, in preparation for the trek back across the world to School House. "It wasn't so long ago" Zepho reflected to himself "that some poor devil had been thrown off the Stairs at the spring rites every year to appease the Sun God." As Zepho well knew, there had been violence as well as peaceful periods in the past but, all things considered, mankind was progressing. The World was indeed now a more civilised place than it had been for a long time.

The school party now set off and the ridges between the fields, which had looked like hoops in the giant barrel of the world when viewed from the Bell platform, now just seemed to be endless parallel barriers to their progress. Zepho never could understand why the soil level between the ridges was so low, or alternatively why the ridges were so high. The teachings said that the levels were lower now than in the olden times because so much goodness had been taken out of the soil by intensive farming, but Zepho found this difficult to believe. Fortunately, the soil was still quite deep enough for all practical purposes. A Farmer over near Happy Hamlet had once dug a huge hole, and found nothing but more soil. It seemed to go on down indefinitely.

The party climbed up an earth ramp on to Halfway Path and rested. Zepho used the break as an opportunity to examine the children on World geography. His gaze drifted over the scattered forms of his pupils, coming to rest on the two whispering girls at his feet. "Come now" he said "Before we move too far from Bell End, which of you girls can point out to me the Hall of Silence?"

The whispering ceased, but neither of the girls immediately ventured a reply. Adam, sitting behind Zepho, exasperated by the delay and unable to contain himself any longer, blurted out "It's back there where we've just come from, underneath the stairs to Hemlock."

Zepho frowned, "I asked one of the girls" he said sternly, "And furthermore you're wrong. There is a hall there, but not the Hall of Silence."

Adam silently cursed himself for being so stupid as to make such a simple mistake. He knew perfectly well where the Hall of Silence was.

One of girls at Zepho's feet stood up and pointed up and back to very top of Bell End. There through the rapidly thickening haze could just be discerned the shimmering outline of the entrance to the Hall of Silence, set in the end of the World near the Village of Hail. "Then it must be the Hall under the stairs to Molock" she announced triumphantly. As she turned and sat down she shot Adam a smirk.

"And what is that Hall used for?" asked Zepho.

This time the girl answered without hesitation, "The Council meet there four times a year. I know that because my….."

"Alright, alright" interrupted Zepho, smiling now and looking around him before going on, "Does anyone know what else happens there?"

A chorus of voices put up suggestions and by the time Zepho had extracted the correct answers and explained them, it was time for the party to move on. They moved off with the children noisily chattering amongst themselves, while Adam continued to fire questions at Zepho. However, it wasn't long before aching calf muscles and feet reduced most of the party to silence. They pressed on to School House, and reached it just as it began to rain.

At about the time that the school party set off from Halfway Path, almost directly overhead, Adam's girl arrived back, breathless, on the high path, above the farm which was her home. Wrapping her leather skirt more tightly around her knees, she slid, in a crouch, on her bare feet quickly down the grassy bank of the path and into the field where she, and her elder brother Abel, had been working all morning. Whilst she endeavoured to make up for her absence with a frantic turn of speed with a spade, pilling the dark soil in rows around the green potato shoots, her brother called to her quietly from several rows away.

"You're for it" he whispered loudly, "Dad's been looking for you. What have you been doing, and how did you get those red marks on your arm?" Her brother grunted as he heaved a pile of weeds from between the vegetable rows. "You've been cavorting with the wildmen, haven't you?" he added hoping to provoke her into a reply.

The girl continued her labours, and replied intermittently as and when she could. "Wildmen aren't abroad at this time of day, idiot …….. I went to Happen to have a message written …………. I bumped into that pig Shepho …………. he's, he's got my message now. Oh, Abel, what am I going to do?" The girl turned away as the humiliation of her experience returned. Her brother, initially irritated by her absence and lack of progress in the field, now regarded her with concern. He hadn't realised just how close to tears his sister had been. Abel was just about to make a conciliatory remark, when their father came striding purposefully from the farm house. Still some distance off he began to shout indignantly at his two young farm hands.

"Look you two, how do you think I've made this farm as prosperous as it is today?" He climbed the reed fencing into the potato field and advanced towards them once again. "By hard work, that's how. Just sheer, muddy, back-breaking work."

Abel straightened up, resting his dirty hands palms outwards in the small of his back, "I have been working hard" he protested.

"Yes, yes, I know" replied his father, "but your sister here seems to think that farming is a kind of part-time occupation." He took the spade from his daughter's limp hands and began to dig great the earth with his powerful arms. The girl stood silently and glumly listened to him nagging at her.

"When this is finished, there's the chicken house to clean out; the pigs to provide with fresh straw; the wheat and rapeseed fields up by the Lone tree to weed" he stopped for a moment to hail a friend passing on the path nearby, and then continued, "There are rats again in the barn that will have to be smoked out and then …… "

Abel interrupted, "But Dad, we've had better harvests these past few years, for all our crops, than you can ever remember."

His father paused and swept his hand across his perspiring brow, "Maybe" he admitted, "but supposing the next few harvests are the worst we've ever known. Then you'll be grateful for the way I have driven you all on. Better to be safe than sorry." The farmer, now satisfied with the quality of his potato field, turned at last to his daughter.

"Now, young lady, I suppose you …….." he stopped as, for the first time, he saw the tears beginning to trickle down the young girls face, "Hrump, oh, hang it all sweetheart, I know that I've been irritable lately, but there's a lot on my mind." He put his arm around his daughter's shoulders, "However, I must make a good future farmer's wife out of you for some young man." His features broke into a smile, "Even if you are, also, too preoccupied on other matters, at present, to concentrate on your work in the fields. Cheer up, there's a good girl."

The girl sniffed and wiped her eyes on her sleeve. "I know I don't always work as hard as I should, dad, and it's not you that's upset me." Her father glanced at Abel but, after a silent signal from him, decided not to press the matter. He patted her gently on the bottom saying, "You go in, dear, and help your mother get the supper ready."

As his sister departed towards the farm house, Abel gathered up the tools they had been using. "Enosh and I can help keep the farm going" he said, trying to stamp on a large beetle. "The three of us should be more than enough."

Abel's father stood silently for a moment, lost in thought. Finally he said, "It's more a matter of training, and of keeping her fully occupied."

At first Abel thought that his father's reference to keeping her busy was to keep her mind off boyfriends but then he recalled that, soon, his sister would be fifteen years old. He did not need his father to spell out any more clearly the ominous implication of this age and the trial she would then have to undergo. As Abel and his father worked their way back to the farmyard, the rain began to fall softly on the plant leaves, the grass and the dusty brown tracks in the garden of the World.

Chapter Two - Known and Unknown

The outer wall of School House stood proud of the end of the World by some seven strides and the door was massive, circular and cumbersome, so it was invariably left open. On either side of School House, starting at a distance of about thirty strides from the School's outer door and following the wall that comprised the End of the World, a lake stretched away, muddy and dark near at hand, but further away to become like a ribbon of silver, meeting high above the Sun on the further side of the World.

Inside the school, it was always cool compared to the outside, and the pupils would sit on the floor with light coming in through the door. The inside walls were covered with drawings and graffiti, put there by centuries of children. Pin men and rude drawings were scribbled everywhere, and nothing the priests could say or do kept them free of markings.

Along one wall, and clear of it by about a hand span, were a series of vertical bars which reached from floor to ceiling. Their purpose was unknown but the priests sometimes used them for exercising the children.

Behind the innermost wall of the school, in a room of its own, a very curiously shaped room seven strides wide but only two strides deep, was an object of great importance. It was here that Zepho led his class, as was customary, after the trip to Hemlock. It provided a suitable climax to the day and Zepho rather fancied himself in the role of dramatic presenter. About midway along the back wall, for a short distance, the wall became transparent. Within the wall and life-size, were the figures of a male and female human, quite naked and lit in some unknown and mysterious manner from within. The male figure had his right hand raised as if in greeting and the female had an infant cradled in her arms. The children, and indeed most adults, regarded this scene as a kind of shrine since it seemed to have no other purpose. Although the statuesque figures always impressed his pupils, it was not those that Zepho had brought them to see.

Down each side of the figures, as if inlaid in the back wall, were written 'Commandments' in lettering that the children thought was beautiful, even though they couldn't read. The capitals were splendidly ornamental, whilst the rest had a lovely flow with the individual letters joining up, in what the priests called hand-writing.

There was complete silence from the children, which was unusual. Zepho cleared his throat and read the lettering slowly and clearly, giving time for the boys and girls to absorb the meaning:

"1.   The Mother World loves all equally. You too should love each other. Mother World carries you, her children, on the journey through life and will, one day, give her life for you all.

2.   The human shape is sacred to the Mother World. Everyone must attend 'Clearance' on their 15th birthday.

3.   No woman should have more than three children.

4.   For six days, at a time, mankind shall labour. On the seventh day it shall rest.

5.   It is the duty of all to pass on the Teachings, Lore and Language without change, omission or addition.

6.   Any object or animal not attached or properly constrained is the property of he or she that finds it.

7.   See that honesty and compassion are given their rightful place amongst the most prized of human virtues.

8.   *Seek for knowledge, from which comes understanding. For from understanding come benefits for all humankind.*"

Zepho stopped, reminded his pupils that they would need to be word perfect when reciting the Commandments in their tests and, after explaining some of the more difficult words, led them back still silent into the classroom.

Once the children were seated at their places, the atmosphere became more relaxed. The usual fidgeting resumed. Adam started the questioning, as he often did. "Where do the Priests obtain their knowledge, Father? They always seem to know things no one else does." Adam had been asking questions all the way from Bell End.

Zepho glanced at the boy sharply, his irritation with the boy's perpetual questions beginning to show. "From the Teachings, my boy. A careful study of the Teachings and History as has been passed down to us from the Beginning." Zepho considered carefully before adding, "We write down our knowledge, and then what is written by one priest is available to all priests present and future."

"Where are these writings, Father? By now there must be many" encouraged Adam.

"There are my boy, but you would need to be able to read for them to be of any use. Which is why the priests alone use them. As I told you earlier, Father Heman keeps the records at the Hall of Silence."

"Why are …?

Zepho's patience finally snapped. Exasperation appeared on his face. "What we do with the writings is no concern of yours, Boy" he asserted, "now shut up for a bit. Let some of the other children get a word in edge ways. Any more of you, and I'll have you scrubbing the floor after school." Then, seeing a mixture of surprise and alarm on the faces in front of him, and realising that he had reacted over sharply, Zepho added with a big smile, "Now let's see if you can all remember what you learnt this morning at Hemlock, and then you can all go home."

Back on the other side of the world, some time later at Welcome Farm, supper was in progress. Chunks of bread and slices of ham were being washed down, with water by the children, and with beer by the adults. The whole family were seated around a brick table on brick stools, for they were comparatively well off. Bricks were very expensive since their manufacture consumed a lot of heating oil. The farmer, Geuel, who had finished eating and was trying to reconcile his accounts, sat opposite to his wife Rachel, who was endeavouring to instil some table manners into her children.

"And why don't you set them an example, dear" Rachel was saying in a plaintive voice to her husband. "When you've finished eating, get down and leave the table. Don't just become pre-occupied with your sums."

Geuel reached the end of what was for him, a rather difficult calculation and turned to his daughter, who was sitting dreamily beside him. "If I sell six pigs for three coins each, ten chickens for two and a half coins each and then have to buy hay for nine coins, how many coins should I have left over?" he asked.

"Thirty four" replied his daughter after only a moments thought.

"Thank goodness for that" said Geuel, "Because that's the number I have here, but I made it thirty two."

Abel, her brother, who had thought that the question had been asked of him, heaved a sigh of relief. Out loud, he said "It'll be so much easier when my sister is fifteen and we can give her proper name. Why is it lucky to wait only in the case of girls, Dad, until after they have passed through 'Clearance?'

Looking up, he noticed that the room had gone silent and everyone was looking at him, shocked. He had just put his rather large 'foot' in it. Clearance was not something talked about, let alone mentioned at the supper table in front of the candidate. He desperately tried to think of something to say by way of apology. His mother spoke first.

"We don't mention such things in public, Dear, never forget that. But your sister's ability to do sums quickly, reminds me that I had a message today from Aunt Mirriam in Hope Village." She glanced at her husband to make sure he was listening, and then went on. "As you know, Aunt Mirriam runs a market stall in Hope on which she sells some of our own produce from here on the farm. She says she badly needs help to run it. She's not as young as she was and uncle Reuben is almost a cripple now." At first, Geuel didn't catch on to his wife's meaning.

"I need Abel here on the farm" he said, "Enosh too! There's a great ….."

"And what about your daughter?" interrupted Rachel, softly, glancing in the Girl's direction and seeing realisation of the implications of all this flash across her features.

"You can't send a girl to do that job" put in Enosh scornfully, between large mouthfuls of bread.

"And why not?" said his sister suddenly coming to life, "Why not may I ask? Aunt Mirriam's been doing the job very well for many years with practically no help." By now, she had worked herself up into her usual battling stance with her brothers. "You boys always think you can do everything better than we girls can."

"Well we can" said Abel smugly.

"No you can't."

"Yes we can."

"No you can't."

"Alright, name something you can do better" said Enosh challengingly. This caught the girl by surprise, but she was not silent for long.

"Sums" she said triumphantly.

This statement resulted in a pause, while the boys thought up a suitable reply. Their father laughed at their confusion, "She's got you there" he said, "and that ability might be useful to Mirriam at her market stall. But" he went on addressing Rachel, "could you manage without your daughter's help, dear?"

The Girl's eyes, shining with excitement didn't wait for her mothers reply, turned and begged, "Please mother, can I go, please, please?"

"Well" said Rachel, smiling "I would need you here one day a week, and ….."

But the Girl wasn't listening now. This was her great opportunity to see more of Adam. He had to visit Hope from time to time and nothing else seemed to her to matter very much, by comparison. Aunt Mirriam was great, and the Girl was sure she could be persuaded to be sympathetic to her cause. And Hope Village was a pretty exciting place to be anyway. There was always so much going on and the village Master, Alvan, was said to be firm but fair.

Her thoughts were interrupted by her Father's voice, "You may go my love, until the harvest, for there's little point in keeping you here over the next few weeks, in your present mood. By then your right to life will have been confirmed, according to the Commandments." Geuel rose from the table and placed his hand gently on her shoulder.

"While you are there" he said, suddenly becoming very serious, "you can give the Master of Hope a message from me. You are to tell him, and him alone. It is not a long message, so commit it now, to memory. It is very important."

Yet when she heard what she had to say to the Master, it didn't seem at all important.

Adam was a moderately good looking and excessively ambitious boy. He was tall for his age, slim, with a square jaw and deep set eyes. He was the middle child of three, of Ammiel and Miriam, who owned a small farm near Happy Hamlet. His Father, Ammiel, had been killed in the food riots of 4275, his older brother and mother now ran the farm and Adam had been sent to school to get an education. At an early age he had shown an aptitude for organising people, inherited from his Mother's side, a flair for fighting from his Father, and a mind seemingly able to establish fresh truths from apparently disconnected and seemingly uninteresting facts. This last skill he had improved with help from Zepho, who, when he wasn't being irritated by questions, had taken a liking to Adam and had taught him how to reason and to assemble his thoughts in a sensible fashion.

At the age of eleven, Adam had impressed his parents and friends by inventing a light code, with which to communicate with his friends across the world. Watching the twinkling lights of other villages above him at night, it occurred to Adam that signalling by flashing light would save the enormous amount of effort daily expended on runners carrying letters on scrolled parchment. Signalling by flag or patterns set out on the ground wasn't practicable because of the haze in the air at the centre of the world. The idea of flashing lights, however, had caught on quickly and, by now, throughout the World, only lengthier or confidential messages were sent by word of mouth or by scroll.

As Adam went home that night after the visit to Hemlock, his mind was filled with the wonders and workings of the World. He needed some time on his own, in order to think things through. So, after supper, wearing nothing but shorts and sandals, he made for the Halfway Path and decided, in spite of his aching muscles, to make one complete circuit of the World. As he walked, his dog Companion raced back and forth ahead of him, sometimes forcing people off the track with his exuberance and large size. Walking quickly around the world, in this way, gave the walker the impression that, he or she, was walking on the spot and the whole world was revolving around them. Adam, still smarting under his recent reprimand at school, was trying to explain to himself why he had found Father Zepho's description of things inadequate. "All the other members of my class have accepted it, why shouldn't I have done so?" he thought. "The description, or rather explanation, of World activity, has left everything accounted for – well almost everything."

"There is just nothing left in the World as a mystery and a challenge, according to Father Zepho. Very well, I'll find something unaccounted for, like the star shaped markings on Molock and Hemlock, and pursue it. Somehow, I will find an explanation for those marks, no matter how long it takes me."

Adam suddenly recalled some of the instructions in the Commandments that had been read out to them, by Zepho, that very afternoon. "Seek for knowledge, from which comes understanding. Interesting instruction, that. Come to think of it" he reflected, "the eighth Commandment, in the wall, did seem to stand out particularly clearly. The others didn't seem to notice, so perhaps it was just my imagination. On the other hand" he thought excitedly, only half believing his own thoughts, "perhaps it was a sign for me alone."

Adam mentally listed off things he would have to do. "First of all I must learn to read, that is clear. But who is there to teach me? Normally only the Priesthood are allowed that privilege. I don't know any Scribes or Priests who would teach me, even if they had the time. Yet learn to read I must."

"Secondly, I will need to gain access to the writings held by the Priests and from which they claim their combined knowledge comes. The Priests' power is based almost entirely on knowledge. They are really teachers now, with very little religious connections. Somehow I will have to persuade the Priests that my access to the writings would also be to their own advantage."

But Adam's train of thought was interrupted, halfway along his walk, when he came upon a procession. In the gathering gloom, a party of about ten people had come across the ridges from School End. Dressed in the customary purple cloth at knee length, everyone in the party looked dejected and one woman was sobbing into her husband's shoulder. "Make way" called the leading man as the party reached the Halfway Path.

Adam knew only too well what that meant. He grabbed Companion by the collar and he knelt as was the custom, head down, until the party had passed. An unsuccessful 'Clearance' candidate had failed to return to their family. The body would, by now, be resting in a freshly dug grave near the lost village of Hill.

Adam continued his walk lost in sombre thought. Companion, sensing his preoccupation, had ceased from trying to get him to throw bones and now trotted quietly at his side.

To Adam's mind, the obligatory procedure of 'Clearance' was another mystery that no one had satisfactorily explained. As he continued the walk his thoughts followed this new tack. Why was this abomination necessary? Why should the lives of all young people be over-shadowed by the fear of this event? The worst deformities were usually allowed to die at birth anyway. As far as Adam could see the power in 'Clearance', that decided whether it was to be death or life, was strangely whimsical in its judgement. On the whole it weeded out people who were physically or mentally abnormal, but not always. Adam knew at least one man who had had only one arm since birth, but had returned from 'Clearance'. Yet others, without apparent blemish, had not survived. A person's character or social status seemed to make not the slightest difference. Long ago Adam had decided that the power was either arbitrary, for it didn't seem to be random in its choice, or it was choosing on far more sophisticated criteria than were generally known. The thought intrigued Adam for the existence of a judgement mechanism in the World that was superior to mankind suggested the existence of a superior intelligence. Even if it were an impassive and automatic intelligence, it might be appealed to, or persuaded to, part with knowledge. There might be other similar but less conspicuous judgement mechanisms elsewhere in the World.

How was it, now he came to think of it, that the sun brightened everyday in the morning and dimmed (but did not actually go out) at night? Furthermore how did it know to shine hotter and brighter at some times of the year and not others? Then there was the matter of clean water. The village wells always produced clean water, even when most other surface waters in the world were muddy and often smelly.

The more Adam questioned the world around him the more puzzled he became. Things he had never questioned before, and didn't seem to puzzle others, now suddenly started to puzzle him.

By the time Adam had reached home and got ready for bed, he had plucked up enough courage to ask his Mother the forbidden question. When she came in to say goodnight, he tackled her quickly and to the point.

"Mother, I passed a mourning party just now on my walk."

"Did you, Dear? I hope you were respectful."

"Yes" said Adam, "but I want to know what happens to those who don't go to Clearance. Please tell me."

His Mother sat carefully at the foot of his bed, avoiding his eye. "Why do you need to know, Dear? Surely you're not thinking of not going?"

Adam lay back on his pillow and carefully formulated his reply. "If I've got to go through the agony of waiting, I've got a right to know why there is no other course" insisted Adam. "Or, indeed" he added "whether there is no other course."

His Mother sat in silence for a moment, "Yes" she replied at last, "I suppose you do have that right. I was wondering when you would ask, in fact."

Adam could sense his Mother's unwillingness to go on, so he said, "I know people don't live very long after they refuse because I've never met one. Do their hearts stop or what?"

"No, dear" said his Mother softly. "The first thing that happens is that they go blind, and then sometime afterwards, they die."

Chapter Three - Ghost Worlds and Wildmen

As it happened, Adam didn't have to worry about how he was going to approach the Priesthood with his new ambition to learn to read. It was they who approached him first, but about a rather different matter. He was summoned by a brief and somewhat mysterious message to attend a meeting on Sevenday at the other end of the World in the Hall of Voices which was set into the wall under the Stairs to Hemlock.

From Oneday to Fiveday Adam had to attend school in the mornings. Sixday was usually taken up with helping his mother with various chores. There was always water to be fetched, oil seeds to be crushed, goats to be led out and tethered on fresh grass and a long list of other minor jobs around the farm. Sevenday was a holiday all day and on this particular day, long before Morning Bell, he was up, packed himself a lunch and was off down the Hope Path out of Happy Village, leaving Companion with his brother Kenan.

On his way he first passed Caleb's rabbit farm, which looked deserted in the dim light, with all the rabbits still asleep. Next came the cotton plantation, with the bushes silent and still. Adam went rather faster past the next farm, which was an apple orchard, since he had been caught there, in the previous Autumn, giving what his father called 'finger blight' to the apples. Then came the farm he knew well because two of his school mates lived there, wheat was the farm's main crop. Then after some low sand hills and a small clump of trees, he passed Anak's old farm where he often stopped and cadged a drink of goats milk, for he was a kindly man and Adam, at one time, had fancied his daughter. And so he continued across the World, until School End began to look small and Bell End loomed larger and larger in front of him.

He reached Hope just after sunbright, when the air was bright and clear. The villagers where just beginning to stir themselves. Queues were forming at the village well and a cloth seller was hawking her wares from house to house both giving and receiving gossip as she went. Turning right, he followed the path along the foot of the Stairs. Above him, invisible, the Stairs climbing up to the Bell Hemlock and, above that, nothing but the sheer end of the World until high, high above him he could faintly discern the other Bell, Molock, and the associated flight of stairs running, upside down to the ground level at Hail. It would be Molock's turn to be rung tomorrow and for the rest of the coming week.

A short distance out of Hope along the path to Hail he came to the arches in the Wall on his left which were the entrance to the Hall of Voices. It was here that people came to talk to the voices from what were called the Ghost Worlds. An elderly Priest called Kenaz supervised the Hall and, although no one was discouraged from talking to the Ghost Worlds, his were an extra pair of 'official' ears listening to conversations however trivial.

Kenaz had white hair and bright red checks. He was a kindly man but a little full of his own importance, since he had acquired fame, not through any particular talent, but because of events which had occurred, during his term of office. Two new Ghost Worlds had identified themselves, one quite recently. This had raised the total number of known Ghost Worlds from four to six and raised expectations of further discoveries. Most of the features of the recently identified Ghost Worlds were common to the other Ghost Worlds and to Adam's World. There were people, and Kenaz was one, who thought that the Ghost Worlds were just as real as Adam's World but that they lay in some other dimension.

Adam approached the Priest Kenaz who was waiting at the entrance. "I received your message Father" said Adam eagerly. "What do you want of me?"

Kenaz led Adam through the arches into the Hall of Voices and over to the stone bench that ran the full length of the wall at the back. Sitting on this bench was a second Priest who identified himself as Father Heman. The second priest was shorter and a lot broader than Kenaz but dressed in a similar ankle length gown but of a different colour. He motioned Adam to sit beside him, and scrutinized him with bright, shrewd eyes. "I am the Chief Scribe and Historian to the Priesthood" he said in a friendly manner. "So you are the young man who gives Father Zepho such a difficult time. Good at phrasing questions, eh? Invented the light message did you? Determined, I believe, keen to get on and all that. Star pupil, well, well, well."

Adam, although flattered, wondered vaguely how long it would take the short Priest to get to the point.

Heman rattled on "I've had a word with your tutor and he is agreeable to your spending a week or two here. It can be a project for you. Excellent idea that. A project you can tell your class about when you return."

"What will I be doing on this project for a week or two?" asked Adam.

"Asking questions" laughed Heman and Kenaz joined in. Heman suddenly became serious again. "Before I tell you what you will be asking questions about, I must first establish the state of your knowledge of the Ghost Worlds. What do you know about them Adam?"

"Not a lot, Father" admitted Adam. "I know that you sit on this bench at about Sundim Bell time and you can hear voices. The voices tell us that they belong to a World which is similar in many ways to this world, but is not this World. Nobody seems to be able to tell me where the voices come from, or how our voices carry back to the Ghost World. I know that the first Ghost World is exactly like our World in lay-out, and they sit in their Hall of Voices to hear us, and that the inhabitants have a slightly different way of speaking." Adam thought carefully before continuing, "I believe that the other remaining Ghost Worlds are slightly different in size and are mainly grass with larger four legged animals all over them in addition to humans. That's about all I know."

"Not bad" encouraged Heman. "About average knowledge. However, for your current task, you will need rather more than that. You will probably know that we can only speak directly to one Ghost World. If we want to speak with the others we have to do it via the first one – that is – ask them to pass on a message so to speak. It seems that the Ghost World we speak to has to do the same if they want to speak to Ghost Worlds other than their nearest. There's a chain of them which has made enquiry about recent new additions very difficult and tedious since they are at the other end of the Ghost World chain."

"Each Ghost World speaks only to its neighbours in the chain?" interposed Adam.

"Yes"

"But we only speak to one?"

"Yes, but the point is that…."

"How do they tell the difference?"

"What difference?" said Heman who didn't like being interrupted or distracted when he was explaining something.

"How does a Ghost World tell which of the other two Ghost Worlds it is talking to?" persisted Adam.

"They have different names, and they talk to them in different halls" said Heman looking uncomfortable and uncommonly like a man forced to disclose something he would rather have kept to himself.

"And why don't we have two Ghost Worlds to talk to?"

"Because we are a real World" said Heman hurriedly and because he knew this was very unconvincing he went on "No, I must be straight with you, we are fairly certain that the other Worlds are real enough although we don't know where they are. The impressions we get of the Ghost Worlds are too complete and too consistent to be figments of our imagination and the voices are real enough. For some time now we have been forced to take them as being real but somewhere else." And then he added, to satisfy Adam's curiosity, "We don't know why our World only has one other to talk to. One day I think we will have two."

"But all this is by the way" went on Heman. "About ten weeks ago, the sixth and newest Ghost World identified itself to its neighbour. Normally a Ghost World commences a dialogue, when its inhabitants overcome the superstitious awe with which the Hall of Voices is often held. But with the sixth Ghost World, it was different. They had been listening to their neighbouring World sometime before identifying themselves." Heman glanced at Kenaz, who nodded. "However, from their early questions they let something interesting out. It appears that most of the humans on the Sixth World can read and write. When this came out, we questioned them further, but apart from saying they had a number of objects they referred to as 'books', which are bundles of writings, they were not all that keen to elaborate. Eventually we had to trade knowledge for knowledge."

"What knowledge did you trade, Father?" Adam asked eagerly.

"Your light code" replied Heman rather sheepishly.

Adam grinned "And what did you get in return?" he asked.

"They told us where the bundles of writings had been found. They were quite adamant that they came out of a room in School House where the human figures are located. Actually the Ghost World people were rather shy of the whole business and we eventually, after more detailed questioning, found out why. Apparently in their World the room with the human figures had once been quite large with the human figures transfixed in a pillar in the centre. Around the walls there were dozens of these 'book' things. But, after some particularly ugly fighting over territorial rights, the room had returned to its old shape and the secret of its access lost. Fortunately, some of the writings had already been removed from the strange room."

Heman sat silent for a moment looking thoughtful, kicking the dust on the floor into strange shapes.

"Have you looked at our School Room carefully?" asked Adam.

"Of course we have" said Heman emphatically. "We have tried everything we can think of. we've tried force and commands. We have tried appealing to Mother World and holding prayers. None of those things got us anywhere."

"And what can I do?" said Adam, amazed at the thought that he might be able to do something the Priests had failed to do.

"You are young, but original in your thinking. Your mind is not constrained by centuries of dogma or preconceived ideas. See if you can find out anything we don't already know from the Ghost World which has these 'books'. See if you can determine whether our World has such a room as theirs." Heman stood up and looked straight into Adam's eyes. "If you find out anything, we must be told – that is our condition. If you do find out how to gain access to those books you will be famous."

"And with a good chance of being allowed to learn how to read them" thought Adam. "Wow what a challenge! But more importantly what an opportunity." Out loud he said "When do I start?"

"Now" said Father Kenaz.

As the shorter Priest turned to leave, a man who had been standing listening outside but near the arches, slipped away through a hedge and into the hop field nearby.

Two days later, at the other end of the World, it was cool and quiet and an hour before sunbright. The water in the lake nearby lapped gently against the island. Small hillocks or lumps made of some unnaturally hard material, bare of vegetation, covered this part of the island, overlapping each other in a random fashion. The highest hillock stood about four times the height of a full grown man above the level of the lake. Water from a recent rain storm formed pools and was trickling its way along erosion gullies between the dark grey irregular lumps down to the lake. The sun glowed faintly overhead at minimum intensity.

Near the bottom of one of the lesser hills a man, naked to the waist, was bent double, struggling with something on the ground which defied his grasp. Nearby, at the waters edge, on a pile of stones placed there many years before for defence purposes, still as a mouse, was the girl Zilpah, only her head turning occasionally as she tried to act as both look-out and observer of what her man was doing. It was sufficiently cool for the girl to be wearing a loose cape over her clothing.

Shobal, still bent double, shifted his grip on the handle of the object which, for a long times, had gradually become more and more exposed as the hard substance of the hill slowly dissolved in the rains. More often it was a fork, a trowel or a short bladed knife, but this object was larger than usual and had for some time been the object of Shobal's secret and dangerous desire. He knew he could find a ready market for it in Harp Village, across the water, from any farmer who wouldn't ask too many questions or take any notice of Shobal's single eye, if the price was right.

The handle of the object moved perceptibly and he grunted with satisfaction. Zilpah watched in the dim light fascinated as her man heaved this way and that, desperately racing against time in order to minimise the risk of discovery. The object seemed to be held by so little. Its shape was new to Shobal, being two spikes, one of which was flattened, protruding in opposite directions from one end of a long handle. It would make a fine weapon, thought Shobal suddenly, knowing that this would add to its value. Meanwhile Zilpah strained to catch the dull glint of its material which, she knew from experience, would be covered with a transparent protective film. In her excitement and concentration she failed to hear the soft footfall behind her.

Suddenly the girl felt a hand over her mouth and strong arms lifting her off the pile of stones on which she lay. The man, named Hori, holding her, growled into her ear to stop struggling, whilst his brother, Anah, moved silently past them, stalking Shobal, who was still unaware of the danger. Zilpah fought desperately to warn her man. She tried to bite the hand held across her mouth but her lips got in the way and she couldn't open her jaw far enough. She tried shouting, kicking and hitting out with her hands but her cape hindered her. However, the man was too strong for her. Just as she thought Anah would be on to Shobal, she managed to kick a stone off the nearby pile.

Perhaps Shobal heard the stone rattle or maybe some sixth sense warned him, and when he turned, the man stalking him was only a few strides away. Hori, holding Zilpah shouted "Quick, Anah, now!" Anah abandoned all caution and ran forward swinging a club. Fury rose with Shobal as he then perceived the second man wrestling with Zilpah and his need gave him extra strength. As Anah charged, Shobal gave a desperate yank and the implement came free almost causing him to lose his balance. In one smooth motion he swung it round in a rising circle and, with fortuitous but deadly accuracy, saw the point of the new tool disappear into the side of his attacker's head with a sickening crunch. Anah pitched sideways under the weight of the blow and never uttered a sound. He must have died without ever knowing what had hit him.

It was some moments before Shobal recovered himself. A bellow of fury from Hori, who was still holding Zilpah, brought him back to his continuing danger. "I'll break your girl's neck for that" he roared shifting his grip.

Shobal didn't waste time replying to Hori but plucked at the tool buried in the corpse at his feet and then ran forward cursing and shouting incoherently. Hori's response was to place the girl between himself and Shobal and then yell at the top of his voice "Ithran, Eshban. Here by the lake."

Shobal's grim smile at the thought of such a simple trick froze when an answering cry floated in from somewhere over to the right. He came to a halt in front of the still struggling girl, threw down the implement and waded into the attack against Hori with his bare hands.

Between them Shobal and Zilpah had just begun to overpower Hori when Ithran arrived.

"Run Shobal" gasped Zilpah able to speak at last. "Eshban is coming and together they're too strong for us."

Somehow they temporarily extricated themselves from Hori, and running down the small beach, the two of them flung themselves flat into the lake to avoid the mud ridden shallows. But Shobal was very tired and before he could swim very far the men on the shore had begun tossing stones at them from the nearby pile. For a few golden moments Zilpah thought their aim would be too erratic, but suddenly Shobal was struck on the neck, and nothing she could do would bring him back to the surface. He seemed, to Zilpah, to be made of clay. For a few moments she contemplated sinking with her man but, in the nick of time, her self preservation instinct reasserted itself and she released him swearing a silent vengeance. Back on the surface and swimming a zig zag course, Zilpah was soon out of reach of the stone throwers on the shore.

Back on the beach an argument had broken out between Hori and Ithran on the one hand and Eshban who had joined them, together with a fourth wild looking man called Onam, on the other. Eshban was very tall with a hideously deformed head, whilst Onam was shorter with no apparent deformity. Neither of them wore more than a piece of cloth around their waists. Ithran had picked up the implement and was examining it reverently.

Eshban was saying "It's no good Hori, the girl will tell of the implement to get her revenge upon you. We will have to hand it to Inga."

Hori, still seething with anger at the death of his brother Anah, watched the girl out in the lake now treading water. "I've been waiting a long times for that tool and I'm not giving it up now. What is more I'm going to kill that girl if I have to wait here all day" he asserted.

Ithran butted in "If you go after her she'll only swim across to Harp."

Hori made no reply but spat sideways into the mud. Then all of a sudden he made a grab for the tool and Ithran let him take it.

"you're a bigger fool than I thought" shouted Eshban to Hori.

"Don't try to take it from me, Eshban" warned Hori. "I've lost a brother to get this. And if I ….." But Hori never finished his sentence for Onam had sighted another group of figures approaching from the settlement end of the island. Soon the waiting, now dejected, party of men were able to distinguish the short bulky figure of Inga and her usual crowd of cronies, Bilhan, Manahath and clever dwarf Dishon. When she was near enough, Inga eyed the tool and the group before her with her most dangerous smile. She was almost totally clothed from neck to knee in rabbit fur, this material being a mark of her status as leader, not to keep her warm.

"What 'ave you got there, 'ori?" Hori gritted his teeth but managed to give a fairly precise account of what had occurred. He ended by saying "We were just coming to hand it in, Inga."

"Glad to 'ear it" said Inga taking the tool and strolling off, with her entourage. As she passed the body of Anah, Inga paused long enough to identify him and then shouted back to Hori "Throw his body in the lake mud."

At this point Zilpah, who had been treading water and watching the events taking place on the shore of the island, sadly swung round and started swimming further out into the lake and towards the low outline of Harp Village. This drama, which resulted in Zilpah leaving the 'Island of the Wildmen' for good, was to have important consequences on events nearly two years later.

Chapter Four – The Library of Books

The Master of Hope, Alvan, was almost larger than life. Within the strongest body was placed one of the best minds in the World. To his physique he owed his position as head of the largest village, and to his astuteness, his current position as Chief of the secular half of the World Council. The Master had an interesting rather than handsome face with hard brown eyes and bushy eyebrows. A large nose but pleasant mouth almost filled the gap between abundant grey hair and a short beard.

In local village affairs, the Master ruled firmly and in general wisely. He was inclined to be cautious in decision taking but, when action was required, the Master was an excellent leader. His strength was legendary and even the toughest farmers, self important Priests and unruly misfits avoided interfering in his affairs or opposing his instructions. In World affairs the Master of Hope embodied the recently established power of the Village communities, as opposed to the more numerous but scattered farming population. At this point in time (the year 4281 after the Beginning according to the Priesthood), Hope was not only the largest of the five currently inhabited villages but also the cultural, and effectively the political, capital of the World.

Two days after Adam had been invited to the Hall of Voices, the Master was walking across Hope to see how a house repair project was going, when he noticed an attractive girl he had not seen before sitting watching some children playing with a ball against a wall. Unaware that she was being observed by the Master, the girl continued to watch a small boy, who now had the ball, her lips moving soundlessly to the well known ball-bouncing rhyme he was reciting.

"Bounce the ball quickly, bounce the ball slow

One hundred tall men marching in a row

Where they are going to I don't know

Clap a hand, overhand, poor old Joe.

>Bounce the ball quickly, bounce the ball slow

>Two hundred tall men marching in a row…..

 The child stopped suddenly as he perceived the Master standing in the shadows of the house opposite. When the child turned, the girl also turned. She rose to her feet and made a little curtsey towards the Master, whom she instantly recognised from her Father's description of goat skin jacket and fur sleeves. As was the custom she waited to be spoken to.

 "Where do you come from, child?" said the Master addressing the girl "Your face is new to me."

 "From Welcome Farm near Happen Hamlet, Sir" replied the girl. "I have never been to Hope before. I think you know my Father, Geuel."

 The Master didn't actually smile, but his features softened and he moved off up the street, beckoning her to follow him. The children had long since started their game again, when they found that they were not the focus of the Master's attention.

 The Master walked with such long strides, that the girl had to trot to keep up with him. She hoped they weren't going far.

 "How is your Father?" asked the Master, guiding her down a side path and into open country at the edge of the village.

 The girl looked round to see who was near, saw no one, and answered.

 "He is well, Sir, and he sends you a message in great secrecy."

 "Well what is it then?" said the Master stopping abruptly and looking at her attentively.

 "He says 'Ten are good and fifteen bad', Sir. I don't know what he means."

 "Don't enquire" said the Master. "How long will you be staying in Hope?"

 "Until the harvest, Sir. Then I must return to help my Father."

 The Master stood still and thought deeply, tapping the toe of one foot in the dust at his feet. The only sounds were the children playing in the distance, and some chickens clucking near by. After a while he spoke again.

"I have a task for you" the Master went on, whilst the girl's heart sank as she saw her opportunity for freedom disappearing rapidly.

"You are a sensible and discreet girl, that's obvious, so I will place my confidence in you. It is not a dangerous task but it may be a tedious one. There's a boy who lives across the World from here, but who comes regularly to the Hall Of Voices. I want him watched, because we village masters think he's being used by the Priesthood for something or other. One of my men overheard a conversation in the Hall of Voices, not two days ago, which disclosed things about which I have not been informed."

The Master turned back towards the village and the girl followed. "Without appearing too obvious, make a friend of him, find out what you can and send me word of anything you learn." Then he stopped and looked down at her. "That shouldn't be too difficult, for a pretty girl like you" he said, and although his voice still had the ring of authority, there was a look in his eye which was almost teasing. As the two of them made their way between the houses it was a credit to the girl that she didn't immediately shout for joy and still managed to sound dutiful and anxious to please, when the Master concluded, "His name is Adam, and he comes from near Happy Village."

Three weeks after Adam's trip to the Hall of Voices, he returned to the School House with Father Heman. Zepho received them solemnly, and a little apprehensively. His arrival at the midday break had caused something of a stir, the other boys and girls greeted Adam with enthusiasm tinged with envy at his long absence from school routine. There was no furniture to speak of in School House and the pupils sat on the floor for lessons. Adam now strode into the centre of the main School room and, with Zepho's permission, unrolled a large piece of parchment on the floor. The boys knelt on the corners to prevent them springing back, and peered at it with interest but clearly not understanding. Zepho edged closer before speaking.

"Well, my boy, what have you brought us?" he glanced down at Heman, "or has Father Heman brought us something?"

"It is a joint effort" said Heman smiling indulgently in the direction of Adam. But it was clear to Zepho, by the way that Adam had brought in the parchment, that somewhere during the past three weeks the initiative had passed from Heman to Adam.

Adam sat back, clasping his hands round his knees, and began to explain in a voice full of excitement and enthusiasm.

"You all know from Father Zepho that I was asked to question one of the Ghost Worlds. In fact it was Ghost World number six, in order of discovery, where most of the people can read and write. They claim that around the Statues and Commandments there once existed a room which contained writings, on what's called 'paper', in things called 'books'. I wanted to question the people on Ghost World six more closely, to determine whether there was any clue that might help me find a similar room in our World."

Adam changed his position and knelt beside the parchment, whilst his school mates peered and stretched their necks for a better view. "The first problem was to establish some kind of link or common interest with Ghost World Six, through the other Ghost Worlds. I did this by forming, what I call, the Brotherhood, one member of which is on each Ghost World, and is composed of four boys and one girl on Ghost World Four."

"And what is this parchment for?" asked Zepho.

"I'm coming to that. Well, we soon had information travelling down the Ghost World chain and this paper here, is useful not only because it became very difficult to remember everything I was told, but also because I had to think of some way of sustaining the Brotherhood's interest in the project. So I have drawn this parchment description of the World which, Father Heman tells me, is called a map." Adam started pointing. "At the top here we have what our World looks like. I've got all the Ghost Worlds to draw the same maps." Adam looked round, extremely pleased with himself, and noted the puzzled looks of his audience.

"What are those lines?" asked one of the boys "And what's that blob?"

"The lines are the ridges which go round the world and that blob is the Village of Hope" Adam explained.

Zepho sniffed "How, my boy, do you represent something shaped like a water barrel on a flat piece of parchment?"

"Well" said Adam. "I've had to imagine the World cut and opened out flat. And I've also had to leave both ends of the world off altogether. Perhaps I could draw them separately as circles …….." His thoughts wandered off.

"Very ingenious" said Zepho. "And what do you hope to gain by the use of this er…. er… map thing?"

"Well, I've found some interesting differences already. For example, it soon became clear that all the Ghost Worlds are shaped like water barrels with us all living inside, although that comparison is wrong in one respect because there isn't an outside to our World.

"Indeed so" snorted Zepho reprovingly; to suggest an 'outside' was regarded as blasphemous.

Adam continued, "Some of the Ghost Worlds are only half the length of our World but all have a second Hall of Voices where we have a Hall of Silence. So they only speak to one Ghost World through each Hall of Voices."

"Yes we knew that" said Zepho. "That is why it took an inordinate amount of time to get a message passed down the chain of Ghost Worlds. Someone had to travel halfway round their World between Voice Halls to pass a message on."

"Well, you may have known it but I had to find it out for myself, Father" said Adam cheekily, but immediately regretted his tone of voice. "Anyway, I have found out something more interesting than that, and it concerns the School House. Now each Ghost World and our World has a Bell End and a School End which are almost identical in every case. The Bell Ends have two stairs and under them the Halls of Voices, in our case a Hall of Silence under Molock Stairs. Now, when you draw their precise position, you find that these Halls are no deeper than the Stairs under which they lie. In the same way, all School Ends have a School and Clearance, but again mainly built out into the World and not into the sheer end of the World. Except for the Statue room in School House, and the very deepest room in Clearance." Adam paused and glanced round to see if his audience was following his reasoning. Then he continued.

"I got the Brotherhood to draw their School End Buildings in great detail, and in all the Worlds there are rooms here which go very deep in the end of the World."

"You mean" interrupted Heman "that the rooms go deeper than the buildings stand proud of the Wall."

"Yes" said Adam exasperated at his inability to express himself well. "In the case of Clearance the deepest room is about seven strides by seven strides. In the School we have something like a third of the same sized room, and I'm sure that the Ghost World Six is correct when they say that there was, and perhaps still is, a full room there." Adam then added as an after-thought "There are some other differences between the Worlds, but these don't seem to be connected with the problem of hidden rooms."

"Then what?" said Zepho who was beginning to be impressed, not because of the findings for he knew about the possible existence of the room already, but because of the thorough way Adam was going about confirming known detail before speculating further. "He'd had a good teacher, mind" he thought, "but would all this help them get any nearer to this room?"

Adam went on again "Now, having convinced myself that the room of writings could exist, we then came and examined the Wall here in School House which, if we are correct, blocks our way to the hidden part of the room. Here I needed the help of Father Heman who examined the statues of the human figures and the writings of the Eight Commandments in detail." Adam looked at Father Heman, as if to let him take up the story, but the Priest motioned him to continue.

"We then went back to talk to the Ghost Worlds about the matter. It is a curious thing that the statues are identical in each world, and so is the substance of the Commandments written beside them. However, the last commandment whilst being the same on five Ghost Worlds doesn't exist on the wall of the sixth." Adam paused to let this sink in. Then he continued. "Moreover when we asked the Brotherhood to tell us exactly what their eighth Commandment looked like in all the other five Ghost Worlds, it appears that the lettering is different to the first seven Commandments."

"Let me get this straight" interrupted Zepho. "You are saying that the World where reading and writing is common, doesn't have the eighth Commandment at all!"

"Yes Father, that's right" said Adam, and Heman added "They didn't tell us of this difference because they didn't know it was a difference. They assumed all the other Ghost Worlds had only seven Commandments."

"And the lettering on all eight Commandments is different from the other seven?"

"Yes" said Adam.

All eyes flicked back to Zepho. "Come to think of it the lettering on our wall is different for the eighth Commandment. Let's have another look." He moved off and everyone else followed falling over themselves to be the first behind him. It would have been gloomy in the Statue room after the School House, had it not been for the illumination of the figures and lettering. It was very quiet and only the rustling of their clothes and sound of nervous breathing gave any indication of the excitement everyone felt.

When the whole party were inside the Statue Room, Zepho examined the lettering and indeed it was different. It seemed to give greater emphasis to this last Commandment than the others. He read it aloud to remind everyone of its message.

"Seek for knowledge, from which comes understanding. For from understanding come benefits for all humankind."

Adam appealed to Zepho "Let me try to open the writings room, Father" he begged. "I'm sure this Commandment is a clue."

"Good gracious no" said Heman from behind. "Why, the Senior Priest is not here, nor the Council. It must be attempted in the proper formal manner and the matter is strictly for the Priesthood."

"Oh just let me practise then" said Adam.

Urged by his classmates "Go on let him;" "He won't do it:" "Give him a chance to try;" "Bet he does it in the end;" Heman looked at Zepho for support. Zepho thought it extremely unlikely that anything would come of the attempt, but at the same time realised he wouldn't get nearly such a good chance to see anything that did happen, if all the Council and Priesthood were brought to attend.

"I don't see that it will do any harm to let him try" he said.

Adam spoke clearly and quietly choosing his words with care, but nothing changed in the room about them. All eyes were fixed on him as he tried again, and yet again. Then after the fourth attempt, there was suddenly no wall where one had stood before. Instead, the human figures were now encased in a transparent pillar, around which a room appeared, along three walls of which were shelves stacked with the treasure they were seeking. In large letters on the back wall was written BOOK LIBRARY – VALHALLA HAVEN. Of the eighth Commandment, in the pillar, there was now no indication that it had ever existed.

Everyone present stood rooted to the spot, in silence, for several long moments. No-one dared to say or do anything which might result in the wall reappearing. Zepho was the first to move forward, hesitantly, to examine the new room and its contents. When the wall showed no sign or returning, Heman, Adam and the other children also began to explore.

And that is how without any great ceremony, the most important discovery in the Valhalla Haven for hundreds of years was witnessed only by two Priests and a handful of children.

Chapter Five – Better Understanding

It was a week after the discovery of the room with the books, now widely known as The Library, and much of the initial excitement had died down. Most of the farmers had taken only a passing interest in the discovery. For the villagers, it was an exciting development, and provided endless scope for discussion and speculation. The Council had met, and decided to leave the matter in the hands of the Priests, on the condition that some of the books were available to anyone who might want to come and look at them. Even this was more than the Priesthood would have liked. There was, however, one snag to the priests' control of the Library, and that was, that the wall would only disappear for Adam. For, every time the Library was left empty for more than two hours, the wall in front of it would re-appear. So when the children arrived for school each morning, the Library was behind the wall again, and had to be re-opened. When Reuel the Senior Priest had established beyond any doubt that Adam was the only one who could control the wall, he summoned him to the Hall of Silence for an interview. This Hall was slightly larger than the Hall of Voices and was used for meetings of all kinds.

Adam was greeted with smiles and courtesy, but he had an uneasy feeling that many of the Priests were annoyed that the discovery had been made public knowledge, and even more so because the Library wall was controlled by someone outside the Priesthood. Reuel, resplendent in a purple gown, quizzed Adam most thoroughly. "And now young man, tell us the reasoning that led to your being able to open the room now called the Library."

Adam, who hadn't stopped telling everyone about his cleverness for days, was delighted to tell the story yet again. "Well, Father, I asked myself why I would conceal a room of books from everyone, and the only reason I could think of, was to prevent them from becoming damaged till they were needed. So I imagined myself wanting to hide something until someone was ready for it, and tried to decide how I would determine that they were ready for it, if you see what I mean. The people on Ghost World six told me that you had to speak to the wall to make it disappear." Adam counted off the points he had taken into account. "First of all I would expect the people to be far enough out of savagery to want to learn more about their world. Secondly, I would expect them to come and ask to be taught. Thirdly, I would want more than a few people to come and ask, to avoid the case where a single genius might come forward, whereas everyone else was still not advanced enough to benefit. Then I took note of the eighth Commandment on the Wall." Adam paused to regain his breath.

"So what precise words did you use?" persisted Reuel, and the other Priests leant forward expectantly to catch every word.

"I spoke quietly and clearly and I said Mother World, my many friends and I come to you with a request. We wish to know more about the world we live in than can be learnt from the Teachings and Legends. The Commandment on this wall reads – 'Seek for knowledge, from which comes understanding. For from understanding come benefits for all humankind.' I therefore ask, not for myself alone, but for the benefit of all, that you give us the means to teach ourselves. And to my surprise, as well as everyone else's, the Library was revealed."

Reuel shifted his position slightly and, waiting for some whispering to die down, glanced around at his colleagues "And do you know, Adam, why you have been selected by Mother World as her tool?"

"No I don't" said Adam frankly. "I think it was either chance that the 'voice lock' accepted my request and thence my voice, or it is part of a scheme to protect the person that asks to learn more for the benefit of all." He looked a little apprehensively at the Senior Priest, when he was making these latter comments.

There followed a detailed discussion about the meaning of the term 'voice lock', which Adam had picked up from Zepho who had been further investigating the Library, after which Adam was asked to leave for a spell, while the Priests deliberated amongst themselves.

Some considerable time later Adam was summoned back into the presence of the Senior Priest and Zepho. Zepho looked very contrite and had clearly had a 'ticking off' for handling things badly. This had been done privately so as not to lessen his authority with the children, but Adam detected a certain pride in Zepho's demeanour – after all, it was his pupil who had made the discovery.

"I have decided" started Reuel, "that you are sincere in your wish to help mankind as a whole. However, you have been a little over enthusiastic in your approach. Knowledge can be dangerous in the hands of those who are not properly in control of themselves. You have heard that the Library is now the property and responsibility of the Priesthood" and he emphasised the word 'responsibility' heavily. "You will have to open it every morning and ….."

"Can I learn to read and write?" interrupted Adam playing the only card he had.

"You shouldn't interrupt me boy, but yes, you can learn with Zepho here, he will be responsible for your conduct."

Adam couldn't see why the Priesthood didn't just remove all the books from the Library and forget about him, but he guessed that both pride and effective control of the books were the reasons. And besides, some items in the Library couldn't be taken away. His thoughts were interrupted as the Senior Priest spoke again.

"The Master of Hope has asked that the Girl, you teamed up with a couple of weeks ago, be allowed to accompany you. I can hardly refuse, without appearing unreasonable. But I don't like it, and one piece of concealed information by you and I will send her home. You have been warned." The Senior Priest felt rather pleased with this, and reckoned it would keep Adam in check, as nothing else would.

As Adam departed in high spirits, Zepho wondered where all this was leading, whilst the Senior Priest turned his mind to how best the Priesthood could use the new knowledge. "If Adam and his Girl became too difficult" Reuel reflected cynically, "an accident could always be arranged. They were not part of the Priesthood and, in the wider picture, expendable. In view of the recent signs of discontent from the population, this discovery had come at an opportune time. It would take many years to teach, even the fraction of the World population who wanted to learn, how to read and write. Meanwhile there were all the other texts for the Priesthood to absorb. Yes, affairs would have to be watched carefully but, on the whole, things were turning out rather satisfactorily."

The next few weeks were busy ones for Adam and his Girl. During the afternoons they sat in the Library, studying their letters and the rudiments of handwriting, while Priests, and the odd villager, from various hamlets, came to read the texts to be found on the extensive shelving. In the late afternoons the young couple usually had the place to themselves. With Adam's dog, Companion lying across the doorway, they would sit and talk of what they had learnt during the day. Intensive learning helped to keep their minds off the grim prospect of 'Clearance' which, for the Girl, was rapidly approaching.

One afternoon, some weeks after the opening of the Library, Adam came in later than usual and flopped down on the floor next to his Girl and Companion. The Girl lifted her eyes from the book she was attempting to read. She flicked her hair back from in front of her eyes with a toss of her head. "I'm fed up with this language learning. It's ridiculous." She complained, "Why can't we pronounce the same, everything that is spelt the same?" She threw the book aside, and began stroking Companion.

"Give reading a break" suggested Adam "and listen to my ideas for a moment or two." He settled himself cross legged and comfortably on the floor.

"Where have you been?" asked the Girl.

"I've just been over to Bell End" Adam replied, "I went to talk to the Ghost World Brotherhood. All the other Worlds have opened their Libraries now, after receiving instructions from us."

"Hadn't one of the Ghost World Libraries been opened before?" put in the girl.

"Yes" said Adam. "We now have evidence of that. It was in Ghost World Six. This time it was found to be nearly empty of books."

"But that wasn't what I went to talk to them about" continued Adam, "I went because now that Father Zepho has explained the alphabet I wanted to test some ideas that I have had about Village names and World names."

"Like what?"

"Like, you must have noticed that in the Valhalla Haven, all the Village names begin with an "H". There's Harp, Hail, Happy, Hope, Happen; and there used to be Hell and Hill, once upon a time."

"Well?"

"Well" said Adam. "In the first Ghost World all the Hamlet or Village names begin with an "I"; and in the second, with a "J", the next "K", and so on."

"And the names of the Worlds match these letters?" said the Girl, following Adam's train of thought.

"Yes, the names are embossed over the Bells and read Valhalla Inn, Valhalla Jonah, King, Light, Moss and Night."

"So, if another Ghost World makes itself known" said the Girl with her interest mounting, "it should have villages with names beginning with an 'O'."

"Yes" said Adam "but there is an even more important point here."

The Girl thought for a moment, "I know" she said, "with twenty six letters in the alphabet, there could be twelve further Ghost Worlds after the Valhalla Haven."

"And seven Ghost Worlds preceding the Valhalla Haven" added Adam, smiling at his own cleverness.

The two of them sat silent for a moment, absorbing this idea. It was the Girl who spoke first. "The Priests must have known about this possibility" she said indignantly. "They have been able to read letters for a long, long time."

"I know" said Adam. "However, I'm not sure that it helped them, or indeed, helps us very much."

"But we've never heard Ghost Worlds in our Hall of Silence" reminded the Girl.

"That's true" said Adam "But, for another reason, I think there are almost certainly some more Worlds after the Valhalla Haven. You remember my interest in the Star markings on Hemlock. Well, questions to the Ghost Worlds have come up with the fact that, on their Bells, there are a different number of stars. Whereas Valhalla Haven Bells have ten star markings, the Valhalla Inn's have nine, Valhalla Jonah's eight and so on. Because Valhalla Night has four stars, the sequence would suggest another three Ghost Worlds where the number of stars is three, two and one.

"We must get Father Zepho's help to contact these Worlds" said the Girl.

"Wow, it would be a triumph, if we could predict not just the initial letters, but the number of Ghost Worlds as well! Now" said Adam "I must see you back to Hope Village before sundim. The paths are wet now and very slippery."

"I can manage perfectly well on my own" replied the girl, getting up and putting the books, she had been reading, back on the shelves.

"What, and miss a chance of putting my arm around you all the way home." Exclaimed Adam in mock indignation. "Not likely!"

The girl smiled. "I knew the offer wasn't for my benefit" she teased. However they left the library a few moments later, together, laughing at Companion's antics in front of them.

Two weeks later during an afternoon in the library, while Adam and his Girl were sitting and talking with Zepho, who should appear at the door but the Master of Hope. Such was his height that he had to bend almost double to enter. Adam, with Zepho's permission, showed him round.

"On these first shelves" he said proudly "are books on reading and writing. There are forty copies of each book, which is why they take up so much space." Picking a book off the shelf, Adam opened it and handed it to the Master for closer inspection. "Just feel the pages" he said. "Paper has such a lovely smooth and shiny surface to it." Adam moved on. "On this shelving here are story books, some we know from legends but some are new, and they are graded according to their difficulty to read." Adam moved slowly round the room, pointing as he went.

"Here we have books on something called Arithmetic, which is all about numbers really and my girl-friend here has had a look at them. Then there are books on things that go on in the World such as farming, building, repairing and how to keep healthy, what to do at the birth of a baby and so on. These books are full of life-like coloured drawings of the objects described, and maps to explain how things work, or what they look like inside." Adam sighed, "The Priests read these books but I can't manage them yet." The Master nodded to indicate his understanding.

"Then, here" said Adam, "are books describing all the animal life in the World. What is strange, is that quite a few of the animals described, do not exist today."

The Master spoke up, "I believe several types of creature have died out over the years. Whether they were hunted for food, or died from disease, and became too few to reproduce themselves, we do not know."

Adam stopped in front of a piece of wall on which was an embossed pattern. "This" he said "is a proper map of the World. Some time ago, I tried to draw one of these, but it was not as accurate as this is. It shows fields there, and the two Ends of the World separately, there and there."

The Master bent down to look closer, "Most interesting" he said, "go on."

"The only aspect of the map that is really unusual is the title, where it says 'Engineers Only' and 'Library of Light Map' whatever that means." Adam and the Master studied the map for a while and then moved on. "These final shelves" continued Adam "contain a large proportion of the Teachings, Lore and Legends in written form. They tell us two things. First of all, they tell us how old many of the Legends must be. Secondly, they provide a check on the extent to which the Lore and Legends have become altered over the ages. In fact, although there have been a few minor changes, the Legends that we have today, are more or less the same as those written in these books."

The Master moved off to the door thanking Adam and Zepho as he went. Just before he stepped outside he turned and addressed the Girl. "Young Lady, your parents want you home. Go back and help them until your 'time' has come. Tell you Father to have 'patience', I'm sure that all will be well."

To the Girl's ears the word 'patience' was said as a reply to her Father's message, but Adam and Zepho clearly thought it was intended to help her Father through the time when he would have to await the Clearance of his daughter.

No sooner had the Master gone, than Senior Priest Reuel arrived in a great flurry, and Zepho told him everything that had been explained to the Master. He eventually left, somewhat mollified, but he was, observed Adam, clearly anxious for something that was visible in the Library, to be kept hidden. Adam guessed that it was something that he, himself, had noticed, but carefully omitted to mention to anyone that he had observed. The map on the wall had a legend key, that told the user what the various symbols upon it meant. There was quite a long list, and most of them were readily understandable. Even the word voice-lock was clear in meaning, but at first, Adam hadn't bothered to check where on the map the symbol was placed, it being clearly the device which controlled the Library wall. However, checking the symbols one day, he found that the voice-lock symbol appeared in other places on the World map. The small symbol was visible on Molock Bell, Hemlock Bell and at two different locations in the Library.

Several weeks later, as the time for the Clearance ceremony drew close, Adam's farewell to his Girl was a difficult moment. They were in each other's arms late one night, outside her home near Happen Hamlet. The specks of lights from some of the farmsteads overhead were reflected in the Girl's eyes as she looked up at the taller Adam. Neither of them dared mention the small, but not negligible, chance that the Girl might not return.

"I'll be back here the very next day" the Girl was insisting.

"Of course you will" said Adam, a little too emphatically to ring true. "And in the next two weeks I shall write you three letters without any help from Father Zepho" he added.

"Well don't write anything you don't want my parents hearing, will you Adam" his Girl said solemnly, "Mother with want to know exactly what you've written."

"And furthermore" she added dropping her head on his shoulder, "I shall cry as I am reading them."

"No you won't" said Adam softly "because you're a brave girl. Now give me a kiss to remember."

During the kiss and during the goodbyes, the hand squeezes and the brief wave that followed, Adam did his very best not to show how troubled he was, by the ordeal his Girl was soon to face.

Chapter Six – Knowledge Brings Danger

Over the following week, Adam took a more thorough look at the Library contents. He examined as much of the past history of the World as he could. He knew from his school lessons that the present structure of society had been in existence for about eight hundred years. Before that came the 'Age of Kings' which had lasted about six hundred years. From there, nearly back to The Beginning was a neat two thousand years of a period called 'The Lost Ages'. So little was known about them, that Adam doubted the precision with which the Priesthood assigned to their duration. The eight hundred years prior to the Lost Ages and back to the very Beginning were always referred to as the Twilight Years, and their existence was only known about through a series of hand-made marks on the wall of the End of the World in the Hall of Silence. It was believed that people had kept accurate records of the passing of time for this period after the Beginning. Try as he could, Adam found no trace in the writings of any of these periods in the Library records. As a result, Adam began to assume that all the Library records were created actually at the Beginning from knowledge gained before that time.

Eventually, he decided to go and visit the two Bells at the other End of the World. Leaving Companion at the bottom with strict instructions for him to sit and wait, he climbed up the stairs to see Molock with the Bell-ringer from Hail Village and saw that the Bell looked identical to Hemlock.

"What did you expect?" asked the Bell-ringer when he finished striking the Bell.

"I didn't expect anything in particular" said Adam trying not to look down by concentrating on the Bell.

"But, I wanted to try talking to your Bell. If you don't mind, that is."

"Mind?" said the Bell-ringer with surprise, "I don't mind, but what do you want to do a thing like that for?"

"When I talked to the wall in School House, it opened into a Library" said Adam cheerily, "so I thought I would try talking to Molock here to see if anything similar happens."

The Bell-ringers face fell, "Well I don't know whether I ought to allow that" he said doubtfully scratching his head, "It might be dangerous and, anyway, I'm in a hurry today."

The Bell-ringers excuse didn't fool Adam, but he saw that he had made an error, being so frank. He would have to wait for another opportunity to try opening the voice lock which the Library Map had indicated.

Just as they were about to leave the platform, Adam recalled that the names of the two Bells were not recorded on the Library Map. When he looked closely at the lettering under the Bell, he got a surprise.

"Look" he called to the Bell-ringer. "What the lettering actually says is not Molock but 'O' Lock!"

"Molock, 'O' Lock, what's the difference" said the Bell-ringer without interest. "Come down my lad, its getting cold and I want to be home early today."

Adam followed the Bell-ringer down the Stairs, wondering what to make of this new revelation, and what actual wording he would find under the Bell, Hemlock. At the bottom of the stairs sat the faithful Companion who was pleased to see him back, and greeted him with dirty paws and a sloppy lick.

On his way back to the School House, Adam stopped to tell his Mother he was going to the library, and would be late back home. When he got to the School, he found Zepho absent but the Library open and empty. This was most unusual, for the Library normally closed itself up when empty. He sat down with one of the early Lore books to see if it contained anything new of interest.

Some hours earlier, in the Hall of Silence, Zepho had stood trembling in front of the Senior Priest. His emotions were torn between loyalty to his superior, and a genuine respect for Adam.

Reuel frowned while he talked. "So we no longer need the young man, do we Zepho?"

Zepho searched desperately in his mind, for reasons to put off the inevitable consequences of this remark. "The Library remains open now, but there is no guarantee that it will not revert to Adam's control tomorrow, or the next day."

"But the wall opened and closed for you, today, did it not?" insisted Reuel.

"Yes, but …."

"But nothing" snapped Reuel. "And on top of this, you think he knows of the existence of the other Voice Locks. We cannot possibly permit him to gain the secret of those Locks. We should forever be in Adam's hands, or to whomsoever he took a fancy to." Reuel shuddered at the thought.

"Aren't you worrying unnecessarily" insisted Zepho. "What he finds out he is honour bound to tell us, is he not?"

"We can't risk relying on his honour" persisted Reuel.

"We could persuade him to take an oath" suggested Zepho. "I'm sure he would, and the girl too" he added.

"I don't like it one little bit" said Reuel.

"I'll persuade him to leave immediately and permanently" said Zepho anxiously, knowing only too well the likely track of the Senior Priest's thoughts.

Reuel remained silent for some time, occasionally glancing at Zepho and musing to himself. "Even if Zepho could get Adam to leave the Library there were still the Bell Voice Locks to which he would have access" thought Reuel. "No, swift sharp action was required and this old man is not tough enough to take it." Out loud he said to Zepho "I want you to take a message to Kenaz for me. Communication with the Ghost Worlds must cease for a while. This is what I want you to say."

As Zepho reluctantly set out for the Hall of Voices another tall priest, also under instruction from Reuel, set out in a different direction.

In the Library, it was getting late, and Adam had stopped reading to think through all the legends and lore that he knew, to see if any of it now made any sense. In his reading, he had come across a reference to the Valhalla Haven, so he was now pretty certain that this was the name given to his World. A name comprising two words opened up the interesting possibility that the 'V' of Valhalla was also one of a letter sequence, but his arithmetic wasn't up to calculating just how many Worlds that could imply.

Companion was becoming restless and itching to be off home. He was a big and powerful dog, and of the kind sometimes used by the Village guards to keep down thieving. Adam knew he'd have to take the long way home to give the dog some exercise. But first, he just wanted to look up that original version of the Teachings about The Beginning.

A little earlier, the tall Priest Jaalam had stood on a raft of reeds in the lake that ran like a ribbon around the World at the foot of School End, and called across to Inga on the Island. "I want four men, and I want them now."

"For what" bellowed Inga.

A personal visit by one of the Priesthood was most unusual. "It had" thought Inga "to be something pretty important to get a Priest off his backside and make the journey here."

"None of your business" shouted Jaalam in reply. "But the men need to be strong. Tell them to bring their clubs."

"Why can't you do your own dirty work" shouted back Inga aggressively.

"It is the time of reckoning" shouted the Priest. "I have a little job for them. Send them quickly, or you may find the Priesthood less generous with your food supplies." He turned away and sat down on a reed bundle to wait.

"What do I care what they are wanted for" thought Inga "If I send some of the rougher ones, such as Hori and his cronies Ithran, Eshban and Onam, it might even save me some trouble if they get themselves killed." She strode away to collect the men she had in mind.

In the Library Adam sat silently reading the book slowly and haltingly, his finger following the place in the text. "In the Beginning was the Master Builder. He was Lord of Creation and to test his powers he created Mother Earth. In order to hold Mother Earth he built the World. Within the World he placed humans in his likeness, but they had to become better and more knowledgeable, before being admitted to Paradise. So humans would not be lonely, the Master Builder created the Ghost Worlds and, to make them interesting, he made them all slightly different. The human journey through life could be considered a real journey where the lore, legends, achievements and teachings are to be passed on down the generations. This journey is but part of the Master Builder's Grand Design. Hope should sustain everyone and, possibly, within their lifetime will come the end of the World and a Paradise of unrivalled beauty and splendour. The end of the World will be preceded by all manner of signs, and when they appear there will be no doubt about their meaning. The human race must then prepare itself for its greatest trial. If it wins through to Paradise, it will be theirs for ever and ever. Mother World will not enter Paradise, but will give her life for the children she has guarded and succoured for so long."

Adam was sitting contemplating this sad ending predicted for Mother World when Companion, who was lying at the entrance, raised his head with ears pricked and growled. Adam tensed himself, listening to the normal sounds of this time of day floating in from outside the School House. It was nearly sundim, and darkness always made the School House appear a much less hospitable place to be. Then, all of a sudden, he heard the stealthy scuffle of feet on some stones outside.

Adam thought quickly. It could be some of school friends creeping up on him, but Companion knew them all and would never growl as he was now. Or it could be innocent villagers, but they wouldn't slink up so quietly. Or it could be scrounging wildmen from the 'lumps' nearby on the Island in the Lake, unaware of his presence in the School. Which ever it was, there was no sense in taking chances. He got up and moved quickly to the outer door of the School House, which was much easier to defend than that of the Library. Only just in time, he ordered Companion back and out of harms way.

As he reached the inside of the circular opening, he found himself confronted by something that was human but grotesque. Naked, except for a scrap of cloth around his waist, the Wildman took advantage of Adam's surprise and with the flat of his hand pushed him over backwards and leapt forward, over-confidently, to finish him off with a club, swinging it in a long arc from behind him. Fortunately for Adam, he was met in mid-air and mid swing, from the side, by nearly his own weight of snarling dog. Man and dog landed in a heap of legs, bodies, growls and yells alongside Adam who, still in a blaze of indignant anger, grabbed the man's club and struck him a stunning blow on the head, narrowly missing Companion's back in the process. The action had all happened so quickly, that by the time the next attacker appeared in the doorway, both boy and dog were on their feet breathing heavily, not from effort, but from exhilaration and ready for the next onslaught.

The figure at the door disappeared, and there followed a whispered discussion outside. From the volume of noise, Adam reckoned that there must be at least two and possibly three men still outside. Still, three men against an armed boy and his dog were better odds than four men and no weapon for the boy. Adam never felt so helpless in his life as he did at this moment. Of all the ill luck to have been caught by armed robbers. In his frustration and anger, it did not occur to Adam that he was the victim of deliberate attempted assassination. The man lying on the floor groaned but, even while Adam braced himself to strike again, he sank back and lay still.

Then everything happened at once. In the distance he could hear shouting, and a moment later, two of the attackers came in through the door together, with a third closely behind. Adam swung his club and the dog, now that his Master was doing the attacking, just stood bristling whilst the attackers advanced. Adam's blow struck home, but was deflected by the first of his attacker's shoulder, for the man was taller than he anticipated. Adam in turn, was struck by a blow in the stomach and, as he doubled up in pain, the club of the second attacker smashed into the wall where his head had been a few moments before. Companion leapt at one of Adam's attackers, and in mid air his hind leg was caught by a swing from the third attacker's club. The dog landed on top of the man he had attacked but swung round with a snarl to face his tormentor. Unable to spring, it lurched into the path of another club swing at Adam, and there was a sound of bones snapping. It was all Adam could to do now to hold his own club over his head in protection, and shout for help at the top of his voice. So great was the noise, and so intense their concentration, that none of them noticed the arrival of the first runner. As the attackers closed in for the kill, the runner quickly sized up the situation and shouted "STOP THAT!" and then turning his head, he said as if to someone outside "Give me that spear, Zaccur, and take the one held by Ammiel."

The attackers stopped dead in their tracks, uncertain as to what they should now do. Should they risk their liberty for the sake of paying off a debt? Companion staggered to his feet, and stood snarling between Adam and his assailants.

It took the wildmen only a few moments, with the sound of running feet outside, to come to a decision. With a shout to his colleagues, one of the attackers charged at the man at the door, and knocked him aside. He found no one else outside, but by then it was too late to go back. Already, across the field, three figures could be seen approaching rapidly, and further off some more, one of whom looked uncommonly large.

Abandoning their unconscious colleague, the remaining three wildmen made off, in the fast gathering gloom, around the lake. Adam sank down exhausted, and shaking, with his arms around Companion.

Chapter Seven – Child Lore

The Master of Hope smiled down at Adam, as he lay on the School Room floor being attended to by his Mother, whilst his two brothers tried to help the dog. Adam was only suffering from heavy bruises and shock, but Companion was in a very bad way. The dog's hind leg was broken but would, if set properly and quickly, heal satisfactorily. However, the two blows that Companion had received on the body were serious, and the poor animal was in pain when breathing and, every now and then, coughed painfully. As soon as the Healing Priest Zerah arrived, and had checked Adam's physical condition, he accompanied the dog on the stretcher back to Adam's home not so far away.

Prior to, and during, Father Zerah's examination the Master had been talking to Adam to keep his spirits up. At the same time his Mother scolded him for not keeping still.

"Well" said the Master. "That was a near thing, my boy! If I hadn't seen old Father Zepho running to the Hall of Voices, I would never have come in time."

Adam's Mother glanced up "Why shouldn't Father Zepho run?" she asked.

The Master smiled "I know old Father Zepho well" he said. "He taught me once upon a time, and I am familiar with his ways. He would only run in an emergency, and I knew of no emergency. That's was what drew my attention to him. Then, when I looked closer, I saw worry in his eyes and I knew something was very wrong. I sent one of my runners on ahead to delay any dirty work that might be afoot. You see, I also knew from one of the boys that the Library had stayed open today, and so Adam had become 'superfluous' or unnecessary you might say."

This was news to Adam, and he began to get a glimmer of what had been going on. The more he thought about the matter, the more angry he became.

"Poor Father Zepho" said the Master. "You mustn't be too hard, Adam, in your judgement of him. If you had seen the relief on his face when he arrived to find you alive, you would not have judged him too harshly. I am not certain he was even partly to blame for getting you into this scrape. He was also, unwittingly, partly involved in saving your life."

"However" he went on "others are not as blameless. We will extract what we can from the man, Hori, you struck and my men now hold prisoner. It's not easy, is it, striking a man just hard enough to knock him out but not so hard as to kill him. You very nearly fractured his skull. you're a very dangerous chap. I must remember never to be on the receiving end of a club when you're wielding it. However, I think your dog will live. He certainly saved your life today. I've seen dogs hurt worse and survive. I suggest you send him to Simon's farm over near Hope village. His wife runs a rest centre for sick or wounded animals and he can recover there in safe hands. The sooner he is back fit and healthy, the better it will be for him and the better for you."

Adam's Mother asked anxiously "But what has my son done to be victimised in this way? Has he not always been a good boy? The wildmen have no reason to dislike Adam and the Priesthood have every reason to be grateful to him."

"Oh, it was Adam they intended to kill, alright" sighed the Master. "He knows something that others would have him keep quiet, or is likely to find out something others cannot afford to have slip from their grasp. I shall have to find a way of protecting him from further 'attacks', or 'accidents' if you see what I mean."

"I have some pretty strong things to say to Father Zepho" said Adam heatedly from the floor.

"No you won't young man" said the Master firmly. "You'll do and say nothing. You are out of your depth dealing with the Priesthood. They can pull all kinds of tricks you haven't even heard of. My condition for helping you is that you do nothing to make tension worse between you."

The Master turned to Adam's Mother "In order to protect your son" he said "I must become his official Guardian."

Adam's Mother was too overcome with all the recent events to make any considered reply, but the upshot of this conversation was that, an informal agreement was reached, which would make it clear to the Priesthood that any further attempts upon Adam's life, would be regarded as an attack on the authority of the Hope Master.

At this point Adam's Girl arrived and, after that, no one would have got a word of sense out of him, even if they had wanted to try. In spite of the fact that she was due to go to 'Clearance' very soon now, the Girl had insisted in coming right round the World to see him.

News of the attack on Adam in School House spread around the World rapidly, and lost nothing in the telling. Very soon, the tale had been enlarged to the extent that one small boy and his dog had defended the School, unaided, against a horde of wildmen from the 'lumps', putting half of them to rout and killing the remainder. Even those who knew the size and strength of Adam's dog were impressed, however, at the boy's pluck and although violence was not uncommon, it was generally regarded as strange that anyone would want to molest the School or its pupils. The Priesthood played the whole thing pretty cool, and went to inordinate lengths to get the Wildman released before he could be 'persuaded' to give anything away. They managed it by invoking a right of theirs, carried down from the days of King Zaccur, whereby the Priesthood could examine any prisoners captured by the secular authorities. The carelessness with which they guarded him once he was in their hands, and the ease with which he escaped, astonished no one except Hori himself.

One thing that did spring from the incident was a hardening of public opinion about the people who lived a 'wild' existence at the 'lumps'. The 'lumps' consisted of a series of small, slowly dissolving, hillocks on one of the two islands in the lake. These, together with the wildmen living there, kept the World farming community provided with a steady supply of new tools, agricultural implements, water butts and the like, and sometimes smaller metallic objects, including various kinds of kitchen utensils. The lumps had once been very much larger but over the years had worn down to a tiny fraction of their original size. The wildmen (and women) were made up of drop-outs, deformities (such as survived Clearance) and criminals such as could find no other place to settle or village that would accept them. Houses existed between some of the 'lumps', made out of a more indestructible mater than the 'lumps' themselves, and it was often argued, particularly by their more vocal, adult inhabitants, that they had every right to exist there, despised by and away from, the rest of humanity. "Otherwise" they said "why would there be houses where no farming could take place." Anyway, providing that the wildmen sold all the collected tools at the hamlet markets, and as long as they kept themselves to themselves, restricting their activities to a little robbery, chicken stealing, and the like, they were accepted on sufferance. However, attempted murder was another matter.

Thus, it came about that, whilst Adam and his dog convalesced, a general feeling began to form in the villages that something positive should be done about the wildmen. The Master of Hope offered to act as host for a meeting to plan the necessary concerted action. Although nothing was actually said on the matter, it was significant that the whole matter had not been brought before the World Council.

The Priesthood huffed and grumbled about it, but were in no position, at that time, to make too big an issue of the thing, seeing how they had been responsible for, the recent attack on Adam. The meeting was fixed for four weeks after the first day of autumn – that was – in three days time.

On the night his Girl attended Clearance, Adam was totally unable to sleep. Two hours after midnight he was still tossing and turning in his bed when his Mother came in.

"I do know what you're going through dear" she said sympathetically, "but you getting no sleep is not going to help her, is it?"

"I can't help it, Mother" said Adam with exasperation in his voice. "I shall never forgive Mother World if she takes my girl away. Never! Never!"

"Now don't work yourself up into such a state, dear" soothed his Mother.

"I'm not in such a state!" snapped Adam.

"I don't mind you snapping at me, Adam" said his Mother evenly, "but you chewed off your elder brother, Kenan, this sundim when he was only trying to help you. That was naughty of you, dear." Adam groaned. "I'm sorry, Mother. You see, since the attempt on my life, I've been wondering how to ensure that you are not the next victims of the wildmen. I was trying to get Kenan to agree to always remain within calling distance of help."

"I know you only mean well, dear, but try to do it a little more tactfully." His Mother kissed him and was gone. But sleep didn't come to Adam any quicker even with the comfort his Mother had brought him.

Just before Sunbright, Adam tiptoed out into the yard behind the house, and lay down on a hastily improvised bed of straw. Until the sun began to brighten and dazzle him, Adam could quite easily make out the Lake island on which Clearance existed. It was nearly directly overhead and, in the past, he had watched the Priest Omar punting candidates across to the island at sundim on the little reed raft. Now Adam strained to see how Omar punted his Girl back. If she walked from Clearance to the raft, then all was well. If, however, she was carried then ….

"Adam, what are you doing out of bed?" His Mother stood at the doorway, sleepy-eyed and wrapped in her nightclothes.

"Look Mother" cried Adam, ignoring her question and pointing upwards, "Omar has just left his hut and is going to the big circular door."

His Mother shaded her eyes from the noticeably brighter sun and studied the island above her.

"Do you know if she was the only candidate today?" she asked.

"Oh, I hadn't thought of that" said Adam in sudden doubt. Then he continued quickly, "But it doesn't matter. I've arranged for her brother to send me a light signal if all is ….." Adam sat up sharply.

"There!" he shouted excitedly. "Didn't you see it, mum. Look there it goes again. All's well. Oh, that's wonderful. Of course, I knew it would."

Adam's Mother laughed at her son's joy and shared his relief. "Now Adam, you're supposed to be recovering from very nasty injuries. Back to bed."

"Oh, Mother" said Adam, "I can't imagine anything better than this to make me feel better. She's going to be called Star, you know. Will you let me watch the 'Dance of Lights' celebrations from out here? I shall blow kisses into the air since I am invited but can't attend. Do you think ……"

As Adam chattered on, his Mother reflected on the fact that her happiness for his welfare was tinged with a little sadness at losing some of her son's affection to this girl.

Once up on his feet again, Adam played a great deal with his younger brother to get himself fit. Even this temporary lapse into boyhood was to prove useful to Adam, for it allowed him the opportunity of refilling his mind with all the child chants and rhymes. The truce words, the elimination chants, the songs and the rude rhymes were all forced back into his conscious memory, and nagged at him for explanation just as did the Lore in the Library books. One of the elimination chants particularly puzzled him. It went –

> Traveller, traveller I know you
> Our five fields are still in view.
> Beacon, beacon, guide us true,
> Silent Partner, out goes you.

Why say traveller twice? What five fields? What were Beacons? Who was the Silent Partner? Assuming it originally had a meaning, Adam couldn't think of anywhere in the World where two travellers, five fields, two Beacons and a silent partner had any significance.

It was about this time that Adams voice finally broke, and with his deeper voice came a greater maturity and outlook, although he never fully lost his propensity for occasional excitable outbursts. He began to see the sense of not raising the matter of his recent experience with Zepho. Both Adam and Zepho knew that Reuel had been behind the attack, but there was little point in falling out over the matter. Their common interests were greater than their differences. Adam realised he was going to have to learn what the Master of Hope called a measured response, and not go wildly or blindly into disputes or arguments. If he was to get his way in the world, he would have to find out how to control his anger.

As the day for the 'Wildmen' meeting drew near, Adam began to prepare for what he might say to the assembled gathering about his recent escapade. The Master of Hope smiled reassuringly when Adam asked him what he was supposed to say.

"Just tell them what you have found and what happened to you, young man. Leave out no detail, except facts which might lead you to a charge of blasphemy. You may be sure that the Priesthood will wish to attend. Have no fear, and speak clearly" the Master added, knowing that Adam sometimes swallowed his words when nervous.

"That won't be very easy" persisted Adam, "because I won't know at what point a Priest will complain."

"Don't worry" said the Master. "I'll help you out of trouble where I can." And that was how it was left.

Just before leaving home to travel to the Meeting, Adam sent word to Star to undertake a small task for him over at the Hall of Voices and, whilst in Hope, to attend the gathering to which he was going. Also, she should be sure to bring some of Companion's favourite biscuits, since the dog was already very much better, and had an appetite that was keeping pace with its good progress at Simon's farm. Adam wondered whether he would have made as good a recovery, had he been as badly wounded as Companion.

At sunbright, on the appointed day for the Meeting, there began to assemble in a central spot in the village of Hope, a group of some eighteen people. The Master of Hope, Alvan, was the Host. Next to him sat his Deputy, Ebal. Next to him were the four Masters of the villages Happy (Cheran), Harp (Aran), Hail (Lotan) and Happen (Akan) together with their assistants, three of whom were women (the deputies remaining in their respective villages). Two Priests were present, Jeuish and Korah, dressed in their formal robes, looking solemn and with orders, apparently, to hear everything and say little. Two Scribes and three Runners made up the remainder of the gathering, whilst Adam and Star waited some way off, to join them when invited.

About an hour after sunbright, the Master of Hope cleared his throat to obtain silence, and began the proceedings.

"Welcome to Hope everyone, and to this meeting. We are gathered today to reflect upon the problem of the wildmen who live on the Lake Island known as 'The Lumps'. Until recently these folk kept out of everyone's way, but now they have become bold, and there have been several instances of armed robbery. Now, even the school boy Adam has been attacked, for no apparent gain, and we must take some action to prevent these forays from becoming more frequent still."

The Master paused, and looked round to see if he carried the others with him. The Master of Hail motioned that he wished to speak.

"I know they gather up the tools found in the Lumps" he said "but why do the Priesthood supply them with food if they are a plague upon the rest of us?"

"To prevent them from becoming a worse plague" interjected Priest Jeuish quickly.

The Master of Happy then spoke "Why are they only now becoming restless? Are they increasing in numbers? Has Inga become an ambitious and fool-hardy leader?"

"No, they remain small in number and, as far as I know, Inga has no aggressive ambitions" explained the Hope Master. "It is my belief that someone or something pushed them into their latest attack at the School. But" he went on rapidly avoiding the eye of the two Priests, "I'm not interested in who caused it, for that we shall probably never know. The three men involved were found dead in the lake shortly afterwards. What is interesting, is what they hoped to achieve and why."

"Perhaps the latest victim could shed some light on the matter?" the Master of Hail suggested.

"Indeed I think he could" said the Hope Master. "Adam is nearby. With your permission I will invite him to join us."

"What has this to do with action against the wildmen?" asked the other priest Korah, who couldn't bear to sit silent any longer. "Surely the victim's evidence is irrelevant. What we need is a plan of action. Come, what do the Masters of Harp and Happen think of this diversion from the main purpose of the gathering."

The Master of Hope used his powerful voice to be heard, at a point where several people wanted to speak at once.

"I wish to show that the incident at the school was an isolated case, and is unlikely to occur again." He looked directly at the Priest who, although about to say something, shut his mouth for the moment. The Master of Hope continued. "After all, we have lived with the wildmen for years without serious trouble, and I think we can again. The alternative, you realise, is to move them or to kill them. Both are formidable tasks, which will bring much bloodshed. Now I propose we ask the victim to join us. It cannot do any harm can it?"

The Master ignored the grumbling priests, and signalled for Adam and Star to join them. With some relief, he realised that a major hurdle had been overcome. After introductions, Adam explained in a few words the reasons for his presence at the School, and the circumstances of his fight with the wildmen. All those present, at the meeting, had heard about the opening of the Library, but were nevertheless fascinated by the description of the Map it contained, and the term voice lock. They were less interested in the Brotherhood created by Adam, but were intrigued by the possible existence of more Ghost Worlds, as suggested by the stars on Hemlock and Molock and the bells of the Ghost Worlds.

Adam continued "I have searched the Legends and Teachings for further evidence but with little success" he explained. "There is still a great deal about them which I do not understand, and perhaps they will hold their secrets to the end of the World."

"None of this suggests a motive for killing the boy" said the Hope Master, before the Priests could make the point. "Did you find or suspect anything else?"

"Yes" said Adam. "The Map in the Library shows quite clearly that there is not just one voice lock in the World, but four!"

There was a buzz of excitement, and a clamour from many people to speak.

Priest Jeuish got in first. "Beware my boy. It is blasphemy to suggest anywhere exists outside the Mother World."

The Hope Mater was tempted to ask about the Ghost Worlds, but instead, he said "I am sure Adam is not saying that. Perhaps there are three rooms like the Library behind the other voice locks." The thought, that there could be anything like an outside to their World, was an abomination and unsettling to all those present.

The Master of Hail shifted the line of questioning away from such hideous thoughts. "You think, young man, that someone wanted you killed before you could find the secret of these voice locks?"

"Yes" said Adam. "I'm sure it's not connected with my investigations of the Ghost Worlds." He was about to continue when Jeuish, detecting an opportunity to direct the discussion to less sensitive channels, said "I have an important announcement to make."

"Very well but I hope it is relevant" said the Hope Master sighing inwardly at the digression he anticipated.

"Yesterday, an hour after Sundim Bell, news came through the Hall of Voices that two new Ghost Worlds have identified themselves as Valhalla Over and Valhalla Pass, making eight in all." The Priest looked around at the effect this diversion was having. Frowns disappeared and some jokes were made about whether, if the number of Ghost Worlds exceed ten, anyone would be able to keep count of them. However, Adam's reaction was very different. He suddenly became terribly excited.

"Are the two different from the other Ghost Worlds, but similar to each other? he shouted.

"Well yes" admitted Jeuish "they are different I am told. The two new ones both have flying creatures and ….."

But Adam wasn't listening. "Beacon, Beacon guide us true, Silent partner out goes you!" he cried jumping to his feet, while Star clapped her hands in time and laughed at the astonished faces of the Meeting.

"Have you lost your senses?" said the Master of Hope with a touch of irritation in his voice. "This is no time for children's games. What do you mean by interrupting us in this manner?"

"Don't you see" said Adam "You all know the children's 'elimination' chant for deciding who will be 'he' or 'it' or whatever. It goes like this

    'Traveller, Traveller, I know you' two worlds one of which is ours and the other the first Ghost World,

    'Our five fields are still in view', five further Ghost Worlds,

    'Beacon, Beacon, guide us true', two more Ghost Worlds,

    'Silent Partner out goes you', one Ghost World."

Adam went on at a great rate. "It first occurred to me while I was at home and playing with my brother. Ten possible worlds, where the first two were identical, and the next five identical with grass fields, but different from the first two. I then thought about the Legend of 'The Beginning' where it describes life as a journey, and the connection with travellers suddenly became a distinct possibility. When the Father, here, mentioned two more Worlds different again, I knew it must be right, although why Beacon, Beacon, I don't know. That leaves the Silent Partner. Perhaps it is a Ghost World that can never talk to us. I'm right aren't I?"

The Masters were plainly sceptical of this interpretation. However, for the Priests it was a different matter. Jeuish made a choking noise, which he quickly turned into a cough. His annoyance at failing to divert the conversation, had been overwhelmed by the probable truth of the deduction, suddenly put before him by this fourteen year old boy. "Oh course! Where else would you expect to find traces of information from the Beginning. Adult Legends would provide a relatively poor medium, for they would be too liable to alteration and whimsical exaggeration. But children love tradition and their lore would come down through the ages without modification."

The Priest's one aim, now, was to prevent any irrevocable decisions being taken regarding the wildmen, and to report back quickly to the Senior Priest with the news. However, the gathering seemed in no hurry, and they discussed the possible meanings of the rhyme till Jeuish thought he would lose his temper with impatience. Eventually Adam was charged, by the meeting, to consider all available child's lore, and report back in eight weeks time.

At this point, refreshments were brought round, and the Master allowed discussion to wander over all the topics touched upon. Jeuish made some vague excuse, and departed in a great hurry leaving Korah behind. Adam and Star were just about to depart, when Star claimed that she had been prevented from entering the Hall of Voices by the Priest Kenaz in charge there. This news stopped the conversation again, although some of the Masters knew about this development already, and Star was asked to tell exactly what had happened.

"There was nothing to it, really" she explained, blushing at the sudden attention. "The Priest Kenaz said the Hall was closed for a while, but wouldn't say why."

The Master turned to the remaining Priest Korah. "Do you know anything of this?"

"It is the order of the Senior Priest Reuel; and that's all I know" said Korah cautiously.

"This has never happened before" said the Master of Hail. "There seems to be some remarkably quick and arbitrary decisions being taken these days. Was it brought before the Council?"

"No" said the Master of Hope smoothly. "It doesn't really have to be. Until now, the Ghost Worlds have been entirely the province of the Priesthood. The rest of us have been far too busy farming, and surviving, to worry our heads about them." The Master paused. He was endeavouring to get his colleagues into just the right frame of mind to take a decision he wanted them to take. It was a very delicate balance of pressures they were being subjected to. "You will remember that our prime purpose in meeting today was to discuss the wildmen?"

There was a substantial silence, then the Master of Happy spoke. "We shall have to go and teach the wildmen a lesson. It will have to be a lesson they won't forget in a hurry!"

The Hope Master cut in "I think the recent death of the wildmen was an attempt to appease public opinion, and prevent any retribution" he said.

"Why don't we instruct Inga to meet us here first" said the Master of Harp, who was anxious to avoid bloodshed if it could be avoided; after all his village was the nearest to the Lumps.

"Perhaps we can make some deal with her" he added.

The Master of Hope put in. "I would suggest a remedy that doesn't even require that. I would put it to Priest Korah, here, that in future we supply half the food the wildmen are given. In that way we will both be able to influence their future behaviour. Do you think you can persuade Senior Priest Reuel of the wisdom of this plan? After all, the alternative is a punitive expedition I'm afraid."

The Priest Korah departed after the meeting, promising to do his best to persuade the senior members of the Priesthood that this was a reasonable request. More important, he took away with him an impression that the Master of Hope was on his side, and had averted stronger action and worse disclosures.

This was exactly what the Master of Hope wanted.

Chapter Eight – The Signs

A few days later Patriarch Eliphaz, the old white bearded President of the World Council and head of the Priesthood, sat crossed legged on the floor in the Hall of Silence. His distinctively coloured robe, lined with fur, flowed round him and made him look fatter than he really was. It had been raining outside, and wet foot prints dotted the dry sand floor near the Hall entrance arches. In front of the Patriarch sat a group of Priests all very, very anxious to please their chief. As he spoke, the Patriarch could not resist showing a faint look of reproof on his face. "Well Reuel, events have not been going our way, have they?" His glance swept the four other Priests present, one of whom was Zepho, as if to get their agreement to his judgement. None of them wanted to meet his gaze, however. He continued "But let us see exactly where we are now. The situation is rather critical but not in need of hasty action. Rather the contrary; it is time for careful deliberation. From what you have all told me, I see the situation as this." The Patriarch swallowed whilst collecting his thoughts. "The boy Adam, whether from ingenuity or just good fortune, opened the Library of books. Part of his success must go to Priest Heman for encouraging him and allowing him to consider the problem without distraction for several weeks."

Zepho put in "I let him go willingly enough."

Eliphaz ignored him and carried on. "In the course of his investigations he formed the Brotherhood with children in the Ghost Worlds, ostensibly to speed up information, but in reality this has effectively by-passed our control. Once in the Library, Adam was astute enough to notice the existence of the other three voice locks, but so far has failed to perceive the significance of the words above the Map. What the word Engineer means, we have some clue from the Legend of Evening Star and Engineer Joe, which must, I think, be based upon some historical incident."

Genuine interest, as distinct from servility, now appeared in the eyes of the Patriarch's listeners. It seemed they were to be trusted with information normally regarded as the prerogative of the Patriarch and his most senior advisors.

"Whilst Adam and others have access to the Library of Books only, we increase our literary advantage for, being able to read, we can assimilate the knowledge the Library contains far quicker than anyone else, and it will be many years before our supremacy is challenged. However, if ever Adam finds his way through to the 'Library of Light' then it may be a different story altogether." Several Priests now had expressions which mixed interest with puzzlement. However, there was more to come.

"Such limited records as we have, from contact with Ghost World Six in the distant past, suggest that this second Library is a wonder to behold, and contains the secrets of Mother World and her making. We know the voice lock, which controls the wall on which the map is placed is very difficult to open and impossible to force or trick into opening. When Ghost World Six opened their Library of Books, so many years ago they failed to open the second door, although the Legend of its existence also existed in their World, and the words above the map gives substance to it." The Hall of Silence was now so quiet, you have heard a button drop. The Priests couldn't believe their ears. One Library was a wonder, two Libraries were incredible. They sat, opened mouthed, as Eliphaz continued.

"You may be sure that everything in this World of ours has meaning, because it was all planned in the Beginning. The reason for the ridges, for example being closer together, but lower near the Bell End of the World, than they are at School End, may not be totally clear to us, although it is obviously connected in some way with the angle of the sun. However, that there is a more complete reason, you may be absolutely certain. The reasons for Clearance and for Libraries, and perhaps even the Priesthood, is similarly obscure, but may one day be understood by those that search for the signs. Just as we now see how the names over the Bells have helped the boy Adam interpret the child's elimination chant, we must now examine all the other lore for information, which may tell us more about the World in which we live. I myself have already found the instructions for opening the first Library in a child's poem you have all known for years. Other clues may also be staring us in the face." Eliphaz shifted his weight and tightened his robes. "Now, by attacking Adam you have alerted him, and the Masters, that he is close to new revelations. He must therefore be watched every moment of the day, if possible, in case he is lucky again, or brilliant, or both." Reuel shifted uneasily at this point, since the attack had been his idea.

Zepho said "You may be sure we shall do that, Patriarch. But it is the voice locks on the Bells which have always intrigued me. Adam, of course, is not aware of the theory that the Priesthood developed, some time ago, that they are doors to the Ghost Worlds. However, this theory, whilst attractive in one sense in that it implies the existence of an outside to our World, is not entirely satisfactory. Why build them so high up, for example?"

"Again, I think we have only part of the explanation" said Eliphaz smiling for the first time. "Zepho, you must search the Lore in this connection with Adam. Tell him some of our theories if it will help regain some of his trust, and make him morally committed to tell us what he finds out. Fortunately, he always seems quite happy to part with his knowledge." Eliphaz's voice now became commanding "I also want the Library of Books re-examined together with the pillar containing the life size human figures and the commandments. I was fairly certain that the figures merely indicate the 'proper' physical shape of humanity and is, perhaps, part of the criteria used by Clearance. However, events during the past few weeks have shown us that there is more than meets the eye in many aspects of the World design. Examine the figures with great care and study each Commandment in the light of recent developments. Report any irregularities and unusual features to me immediately."

"Incidentally Kenaz" said Eliphaz "you can let everyone use the Hall of Voices and talk to the Ghost Worlds. I cannot see there being any advantage in preventing talk between Worlds, and it only irritates the people, and will cause their sympathy and goodwill towards us to decline. I know, Jeuish, you were going to use it as a lever against the village Masters, but it was turned against you at the Meeting the other day."

Eliphaz took a sip from a cup at his elbow before continuing. "And that brings us to a more sinister matter. There are minds at work, in the World, endeavouring to upset the delicate balance between your authority and the Village authorities. I originally suspected the Master of Hope, but now I am not so sure. The way he modified the conclusions of that Meeting the other day, leads me to suspect that he sees the value of the current balance of power. Either that or he is a lot more cunning and ambitious than I would give him credit for. The Master of Hail is probably behind the matter, and if so he has every reason to be pleased with his planning so far. Our control of the wildmen has been neutralised through a dual food supply arrangement; a meeting has been held, at which decisions were taken on matters affecting the whole World, without recourse to the Council and no one seems at all surprised; the village Masters have acted in unison; and the Priesthood image has taken a knock, over the unsatisfactory way in which we have discharged our responsibilities in looking after the School House and the Hall of Voices."

The Senior Priest Reuel broke in. "What would you suggest by way of countering these trends, Patriarch?"

"In the first place I would propose a meeting of the whole Priesthood. Ostensibly this would be to co-ordinate the dissemination of knowledge found in the Library of Books. There is an opportunity to do this, without being too conspicuous, just before Harvest Day in three weeks time. There, you can inform the whole Priesthood of developments and gauge the strength of our position with the farming community. This manifestation of Priesthood solidarity will not be lost on the village Masters. I'll also have a word with the Master of Hope, and see whether some of the purpose behind the Master of Hail's activities can't be discerned."

The Patriarch stood up, implying that the meeting was over, and waited for the others to do likewise. "I won't attend your gathering before Harvest Day in order to retain some measure of independence and impartiality in the eyes of the people." Reuel, Zepho, Jeuish and Mizzah bowed low. "May you live to see the signs."

As the Priests returned the courtesy and departed, Eliphaz wondered, as many had done before him, whether the events of that year were in fact the signs referred to in that traditional salutation.

SOMEWHERE A LONG WAY AWAY, OUT OF ALL KNOWLEDGE AND COMPREHENSION OF THE INHABITANTS OF THE VALHALLA HAVEN, A

MACHINE HUNG APPARENTLY MOTIONLESS AND SILENT IN THE VASTNESS OF INTERSTELLAR SPACE, MATCHING EXACTLY THE HUGE SPEED OF ITS COMPANIONS. LIKE ITS TWENTY FOUR SISTER MONITOR MACHINES, IT WAS HUGE BY HUMAN STANDARDS, AND HAD THERE BEEN ANY EYES TO SEE IT, THEY WOULD HAVE SEEN THE STARLIGHT SHINE UPON ITS DULL GREY SURFACES, GIVING IT A SINISTER WAR-LIKE APPEARANCE. HOWEVER, IT WAS NOT, AT THAT MOMENT, WAR MINDED, ALTHOUGH IT HAD THAT CAPABILITY. IT WAS AWAKE, ALTHOUGH IT COULD NOT BE CONSIDERED ALIVE, FOR ITS SOPHISTICATED CONTROL CIRCUITS PERMITTED IT TO SEND THE OCCASIONAL COMMAND SIGNAL WHEN CERTAIN VALUES WITHIN ITS BRAIN REACHED PREDETERMINED LEVELS. AT ALL OTHER TIMES, AS IT HAD FOR THOUSANDS OF YEARS IN THE PAST AND WOULD FOR HUNDREDS OF YEARS INTO THE FUTURE, THE MACHINE SCANNED THE WHOLE OF THE RADIATION SPECTRUM REACHING ITS POWERFUL ANTENNA, AND WAITING FOR JUST THE RIGHT MOMENT TO FULFILL ITS PURPOSE. APPROXIMATELY EVERY THIRTY LIGHT YEARS THE MACHINE WOULD TEMPORARILY PUT ASIDE ITS PASSIVE MONITORING AND OBSERVER ROLE, AND BEGIN A SEARCH AMONGST THE STARS AHEAD. IT WOULD SEARCH FOR QUITE SPECIFIC SIGNS, ANALYSING, CHECKING, SWEEPING AND SEARCHING, ALWAYS SEARCHING. THIS ACTIVITY THE MACHINE WAS ENGAGED IN NOW.

FOR THE SECOND TIME, IN AS MANY WEEKS, THE MACHINE ACTED UPON INFORMATION RECEIVED. NO RELAYS SNAPPED OR CLICKED, NO MECHANICAL DEVICES SWIVELLED TO REDIRECT THE MESSAGE, FOR THIS WAS A MACHINE WITH NO MOVING PARTS WHATEVER. HOWEVER, ELECTRIC CHARGES BUILT UP, CURRENT FLOWED AND THREE OF ITS SISTER MACHINES, EACH ONE A HUNDRED THOUSAND MILES ASTERN OF THE OTHER, CROSS CHECKED THE DATA SUPPLIED. THEY ALL REACHED THE SAME ANSWER, AND A COMMAND WAS SENT OUT TO THE VALHALLA

HAVEN AND NINE OTHER VESSELS. SUCH WAS THE NATURE OF THE COMMAND THAT IT WAS QUITE IRREVERSIBLE. THE DIE WAS CAST AND THE FOUR THOUSAND HUMAN LIVES AFFECTED WERE COMMITTED TO THE MACHINE'S CHOICE. WITHOUT A SECOND THOUGHT OR DOUBT, WITHOUT A FAREWELL OR REGRET, THE GIANT AND NON HUMAN SHEPHERDS HENCEFORTH TOTALLY IGNORED THE VALHALLA HAVEN AND HER COMPANIONS, AND ESCORTED THE REMAINDER OF THEIR HURTLING CHARGES ON THROUGH THE VACUUM BETWEEN THE STARS.

It was midday, and the sun shone down as it had always done. The water in the nearby lake looked cool and inviting. Smoke drifted up from a nearby farm chimney. The countryside seemed to be asleep, the only sign of movement was the brightly coloured butterflies in the nearby rape field, and a goat champing at the grass on the one of the world ridges.

"It seems to me that we ought to investigate the old stories, in addition to the child chants and recitations" said Adam to Star. The two of them were seated in the middle of a group of children, just outside Happy Hamlet, who were wondering vaguely why anyone as old as Adam should be wanting to examine Lore in this detail.

"I think" said Adam "we have got as much as we are going to get out of that original elimination chant and, although I don't understand what beacons are, the children are getting restless." A couple of rabbits, watching them from their holes in a nearby bank, reminded Adam that he must tell farmer Caleb that some of his stock had escaped. Adam's thoughts returned to the present. "Tell us the story of Evening Star and Engineer Joe."

"I wonder what 'Evening' and "'Engineer' mean" thought Adam, "I must look them up in the library if I can."

Star glanced round at her audience. They seemed to think a story was a good idea, and settled down to listen. One or two of the older girls played Bob-stones, while the other children just lay or sat with their eyes closed. Star began.

"Once upon a time there lived, somewhere in the World, a most beautiful girl. Her name was Evening Star, and unlike many beautiful girls, she was lucky enough to be born with brains as well, and you cannot get much luckier than that. Amongst her many natural abilities (that is skills one can do easily that others find difficult), was a particularly fine singing voice, and she used to entertain the village on Sixday nights and festival days, although in those days there were no Celebration Day as we know it now, and no bells to ring out the quarter days."

Adam asked "Was she good at kis…."

"Don't interrupt" snapped Star, feigning indignation. "Do you want to hear the story, or don't you?" She continued without waiting for a reply. "Now, in the nearest village, there lived a young man called Engineer Joe. He was bright, not very handsome and unfortunately thought much too much of himself. He was constantly boasting about what he could do, and didn't have a very high opinion of anybody else. Evening Star, surprisingly, rather liked him because although he was conceited, he was kind, when the mood took him, and certainly more enterprising than the other men in her village.

One day, when he was about eighteen and being particularly full of drink, he boasted that he could put a rope across the World and climb up it. His comrades decided to teach him a lesson, and challenged him to make good his claim. This sobered him up very quickly, but he very soon set to make a rope that was long enough to go right across the World. It took him quite some time, but his friends helped him, and the day arrived when all was ready and the rope was tightened across the centre of the World.

Now the Sun had been watching all the preparations with some interest. When he understood what was about to happen, he thought to himself "These humans are getting too big for their sandals. This space, up here in the centre of the World, is my space. Not even Mother World has any dominion over me here. I shall have to stop this young man, or I shall have humans climbing all over me."

So, it came about that when Engineer Joe, encouraged by the shouts of his friends, started to climb the rope, the Sun did its best to burn through it. However, Engineer

Joe had stretched his rope across the World at the end away from the Sun simply because he hadn't wanted to get burnt, so the sun was unable to have much effect. He puffed himself up and shone as hot as he possibly could, but to no avail. In the end, he over-heated himself, and decided in the middle of the day time to go home to the place where the Sun retires at night, and go to bed.

When this happened, all the people in the World became alarmed. They said it was all Engineer Joe's fault. They said that he would have to go and apologise to the Sun, and stop these silly tricks with ropes. In fact, in their worry about the Sun's disappearance, they said some very hurtful things to Engineer Joe, and he in return said it wasn't his fault, and used a few words to describe the people which he afterwards regretted, for he was basically a kind young man.

Anyway the upshot of this was that Engineer Joe was sent to apologise to the Sun, but when he had been gone a week and there was no sign of him returning, everybody wished they hadn't been so hasty. However, they were still very worried about the absence of the Sun. When Evening Star offered to go and look for him, everyone except her parents thought it was an excellent idea, and offered to provide all manner of presents to appease the Sun. However, as she pointed out, she would have to climb the rope to get to the sun, so she took nothing but a few provisions and a number of candles, together with a fire stone in a bag strapped around her waist.

Now the Sun lives in a very dark place. Whilst shining brightly all day it likes to retire to complete darkness to rest. Evening Star had therefore to light a candle every yard of the way, and leave it on the ground. In this way, she could see around her, and also find her way back into the World afterwards. When she arrived at the place where the sun slept, she found Engineer Joe sitting looking glum because he had not known the way back, having forgotten to take any candles with him.

"I've said I'm sorry" said Engineer Joe. "But the Sun says he can't be bothered to go back yet. And anyway, what assurance does he have that humans will stay with their feet on Mother World in future?"

"Well "said Evening Star. "We can solve that last point when we get the Sun back into the World." So saying she went and sat some way off and began to sing quietly but clearly. After a very short while the Sun woke up. "That's very nice" he said "It reminds me of a girl I used to hear singing in the fields of the World. Now I hear it again, it reminds me how much I miss the noises and goings on I used to hear and see, whilst shining down. Perhaps I'll go back and see whether they have learnt any sense."

Engineer Joe and Evening Star raced back to the World so fast, they didn't have time to even blow out the candles. Everyone was overjoyed to see them and even more pleased to see the Sun again for, even though they had been quick, the Sun had been quicker being used to the journey. As soon as she reached the ground Evening Star shouted up to the Sun, who listened to hear her proposal and blinked approval. The Sun disappeared once more, but was back again shortly with two bells, which he stuck on the end of the World opposite to his.

"How useful" everyone said "And how kind to bring us a present, and put our minds at rest over any possible bad feeling between us."

"If you come up here again, I shall take the bells away" winked the Sun, and Engineer Joe translated the message having had time to learn a little of its language, when he was stuck in the dark of the Sun's resting place with nothing to do.

"And Engineer Joe went up to the Patriarch of the World, and asked for steps to be built up to the Bells. And when they were built the Bells were struck. "Is that alright" shouted Engineer Joe.

"Fine" winked the Sun "But please ask Evening Star to sing again."

"And this is why" said Star coming to the end of her story "The Bells are rung every quarter day for the people, and for several hours on Celebration Day, which was chosen to honour the occasion, and remind everyone that the middle of the World belongs to the Sun. And when, on that commemoration day, the Bells have been rung a girl, chosen for her quality of voice, goes up the stairs and sings to the Sun. This keeps him very happy and shining brightly."

"What happened between Engineer Joe and Evening Star?" asked one of the smaller girls who always liked a happy ending.

"Well, they got married on the first Celebration Day and lived happily ever after. Engineer Joe wasn't nearly so conceited and boastful after that. I think the fact that

Evening Star never told anyone how he had got lost, must have something to do with his change of attitude."

"He could have found his way back if he had really tried, couldn't he?" said a little boy anxiously.

"Of course he could" said Adam, smiling to himself. "Well, I don't know what to make of that story, except that I was always told that the star marks on Hemlock and Molock are to remind us of the candles that Evening Star had to leave behind."

"That's a nice thought" said Star, "I must remember that. Somehow, I think the story reflects something that really did happen a long time ago. I wonder if we shall ever know."

Adam sat lost in thought, while Star sent the children off home with a wave and a goodbye.

ALMOST INSTANTLY AFTER RECEIVING THE REQUIRED SIGNAL THE VALHALLA HAVEN's CONTROL CIRCUITS HAD AWOKEN AND TAKEN VARIOUS NECESSARY ACTIONS. ONCE AGAIN NO MOVING PARTS WERE INVOLVED BUT MAGNETIC FIELDS BEGAN TO BUILD UP: RADIO LINKS WERE FORMED AND INTERLOCKING COMMON CONTROLS ESTABLISHED BETWEEN THE VALHALLA SERIES VESSELS: METAL AND OTHER HARDER MATERIALS BEGAN TO GLOW WITH HEAT. AT THE SAME TIME A HUGE QUANTITY OF DATA WAS TRANSMITTED BACK DOWN THE PATH ALONG WHICH THE VESSELS WERE TRAVELLING. THE VALHALLA HAVEN'S MASTER COMPUTER BEGAN TO CALL FROM ITS VERY CONSIDERABLE MEMORY, LARGE DIAGNOSTIC AND CHECKING ROUTINES, WHICH WERE NEEDED TO EXAMINE THE INNUMERABLE MACHINES SOON TO BE USED. SINCE MOST CIRCUITS WERE TRIPLICATED, IF NOT QUADRUPLICATED, FOR SAFETY, EVERYTHING WAS FOUND TO BE AS ITS DESIGNERS HAD INTENDED.

Star's voice broke in on Adam's thoughts. "There was an interesting ball song being sung in Hope, when I arrived there, to stay with my Aunt. I used to sing it myself, when I was younger. Talking about Engineer Joe has just reminded me. It goes like this" and she began to chant, in a rhythmic fashion, as if she was bouncing an imaginary ball –

"Bounce the ball quickly, bounce the ball slow
One hundred tall men marching in a row.
Where are they going to I don't know
Clap a hand, overhand, poor old Joe.

Bounce the ball quickly, bounce the ball slow
Two hundred tall men marching in a row.
One or two above them, one or two below
Clap a hand, overhand, poor old Joe.

Bounce the ball quickly, bounce the ball slow
Three hundred tall men marching in a row.
Daddy can you tell me how came they to be so
Clap a hand, overhand, poor old Joe.

Bounce the ball quickly, bounce the ball slow
Four hundred tall men marching in a row.
Everybody put them there and watched them grow
Clap a hand, overhand, poor old Joe.

Bounce the ball quickly, bounce the ball slow
Five hundred tall men marching in a row.
Count upon your fingers when they come and go
Clap a hand, overhand, poor old Joe.

Bounce the ball quickly, bounce the ball slow
Six hundred tall men marching in a row.
Good luck everyone, Paradise ho
Clap a hand, overhand, poor old Joe.

Bounce the ball quickly, bounce the ball slow
Seven hundred tall men marching in a row.
Caravan to nowhere, makes a pretty show
Clap a hand, overhand, poor old Joe."

Star sat silent for a moment. "That's all there is" she said.

Adam opened his eyes, "Well I can understand the bit about Poor Old Joe. At least I suppose that's Engineer Joe" he mused. "But what is all this marching men business. These chants seem to be reliable when it comes to numbers. Seven hundred what, I wonder. It couldn't possibly be Ghost Worlds, for that would be ridiculously huge and we ………. Just a moment, Star, I've just remembered. Do you recall that, at one time, we thought there might be as many Ghost Worlds as letters of the Alphabet, because of the name's initial letters?"

"Yes" said Star "but that's only twenty six not seven hundred."

"I know, but what would happen if the V of Valhalla changed every twenty six worlds into W and then an X and so on?"

Star thought for about a moment "It would come to 676."

"Mother World!" said Adam in an awed voice. "Do you think we're right? Could there be that number of Ghost Worlds, and why are they said to be marching?"

The Girl was silent for some time. "What exactly is a Caravan?" she asked.

EVERYTHING WAS READY. ALL CIRCUITS, MACHINES, TRANSMITTERS, ENGINES, AND CONTROL SURFACES WERE CHECKED, WITH ONE EXCEPTION, THEY HAD BEEN FOUND TO BE IN PROPER WORKING ORDER.

THE MASTER COMPUTER CLEARED ITS IMMEDIATE MEMORY, AND DELEGATED ITS MONITORING ACTIVITIES TO NUMEROUS SLAVE COMPUTERS.

IT ELECTRONICALLY REACHED OUT, AND TOOK CONTROL OF MANY HITHERTO COMPLETELY AUTOMATIC FUNCTIONS WITHIN THE VESSEL, AND MADE ALIVE THE EXTENSIVE EQUIPMENT WITHOUT. THE RAPID COMPUTER MIND WAITED A COMPARATIVE ETERNITY, WHILST THE INITIAL VALUES OF A NUMBER OF REGULATORY COMPONENTS WERE RECORDED. FINALLY THE PROGRAMME ROUTINE 'SLOW DOWN' WAS CALLED, THE DESIGNATED STAR CO-ORDINATES FED IN, AND THE EXECUTION COMMENCED.

Adam was lying in bed thinking through the day's events. Earlier just before sundim, he and Star had been to the Library, to find a book which gave the meaning of words. The meaning of 'Evening' was given as the period of time just before sundim, as was the term 'Engineer' being someone who repairs or maintains things. There was no reference to anything called a Caravan, but that did not unduly surprise them, for there were quite a number of words in the Legends and Teachings that no one could interpret. Indeed, it was the very existence of these words, which perpetuated belief in the superiority of the Master Builder. Zepho had been sceptical of the theory about there being seven hundred Ghost Worlds, and together they had been trying to develop another explanation for the chant. Adam now lay with his mind brim full of ideas. "It clearly described the start of a journey" he thought "and it fits the journey through life well because it talks about going to Paradise. Why was this Caravan thing going nowhere? Oh well it was no use worrying about it now. Better get some sleep."

Adam was about to drop off to sleep, when something rolled across the floor of his room. At first, he thought it was a field mouse and then, realising that field mice didn't roll, he sat up in bed and listened. It was a small stone that was rolling, but something was very wrong. There were faint creaking's from the walls of the house. If he hadn't known better, he would have sworn that the normally flat floor was tilted towards the door. It was tilted! Merciful Haven, what had happened! Was he having a nightmare? Then Adam heard shouts from outside, and he stumbled out into the night, to find a World that had changed dramatically.

One moment, everything had been perfectly normal. The next moment, the whole world had reared up towards Bell End and sloped away down to School End. In the dusk, people were stumbling about, crying to each other in terror and astonishment. Nearby, a man could be seen jumping off the high path on one of the ridges round the World, water was draining off the fields and up against the ridges between them. Women, with their children in their arms, rushed out of several houses, in the fear that they would fall down. Adam couldn't see the lake from where he stood, but could well imagine what would be happening there, the waters receding from the nearest shore and piling up against School End.

It started as a whisper with the children, slowly gathered momentum as a murmur amongst the adults, and culminated as a shout, drowning all other noises.

"The Signs! The Signs! The Signs!"

"They have come, oh Mother World protect us."

"Where are the Priests, to tell us what will happen next?"

"Oh, the Signs at last!"

During the long history of the World, whenever there had been some great natural tragedy, there were shouts similar to those now heard. So that, although on every previous occasion the claims had been the same, the difference this time was that the people were right.

Chapter Nine – The Library of Light

When nothing further happened to the World in the remaining night hours, most people became slightly less hysterical. No one had any sleep as men, women and children, whose concept of slope was limited to their knowledge of the ramps up from the fields on the high ridges, now had to arrange their lives so as to be comfortable, living on the side of a hill. However, the slope was not very steep, and the animal population hardly took any notice of the change at all. Strangely enough, it was the inside of the houses which required the greatest alterations. Tables and cupboards had to be re-aligned, beds re-orientated, walls braced and hanging ornaments and curtains adjusted. When considered in retrospect, the change was small enough, but a long and firmly held belief had been suddenly shattered. The very foundation of the World had been seen to move, and what had happened once, could happen again, at any time. Quite apart from the sheer physical major inconveniences of the change, some houses had to be rebuilt, drainage channels dug, etc., there was administered to the entire World population, a deep psychological shock. None of the subsequent events, many of them more dramatic than this first change, had quite such a profound impact on society. With the coming of the 'signs', the concept of permanence and material stability died, and, with the passing of physical stability, went a considerable decline in social stability.

Adams reaction to the 'signs' was typical of the young man. After the initial shock, which everyone experienced, and he had checked to see that his mother and brothers were okay, he rushed off to find Star. Adam found her trying to calm her own parents and, as soon as he could, he extracted her from the farm and they both went and stood on the nearby ridge. School had been cancelled for the day. Adam gazed up towards Bell End, and then down to School End.

"This is absolutely amazing" he said excitedly, "Nothing that used to be directly overhead, is now directly overhead. I hope it's all part of the Master Builders' plan. What do you think has happened?"

"I don't know" said Star slowly, "I wonder if it has happened before?"

"I wonder if we can expect further signs?" added Adam. "And even more important is why has it happened?"

"Do you think this is to be the End of the World" asked Star.

"I've no idea" replied Adam, "but if it is, I want to be ready for it. The trouble is, I don't know what to do about it." Adam continued with his speculation and thoughts out loud. But Star wasn't listening anymore. Something odd had occurred to her, and demanded an explanation.

"Adam, at midday today, let's walk around the World along the halfway path. I've noticed something weird."

"What's weird?"

"Wait until midday, and I'll tell you" said Star mysteriously. Curious as he was, he let the matter drop until the midday break. At the sound of the noon bell the two of them walked to halfway path and then set off round the World. On the way, they passed many friends and acquaintances, all of whom wanted to stop and talk about the change. It was only with great difficulty that the two youngsters managed to free themselves from everlasting questions, and continued until they were exactly half way round the World.

Star stopped and looked up and down the World.

"Don't you see what's weird?" she said

"No" replied Adam, "it's just the same here as on the other side of the World – a slope up towards Bell End, except that the half-way path is no longer directly overhead."

"That's precisely what's weird" she replied, "Don't you see, if the slope up to Bell End, from all points around the world really was a hill, then Bell End would have to be smaller than School End!"

Adam thought about this for a bit "Yes" he said slowly "I see now what you mean. You can't have a slope up on every side of the World at the same time. That is weird. you're absolutely right."

Adam and Star argued about how this could be, all the way round the rest of the World and back to where they had started out. When they got back to Star's home they were still arguing.

By mid afternoon on the following day, the worry and dismay became panic, when it was confirmed that the sun was not going to become as bright, as was usual, for that time of the year. This was a change that could not be shrugged off by anyone, especially the farming community which made up the majority of the Valhalla Haven's population. It was true that much of the Summer Harvest was gathered in, but the autumn crops would be bound to suffer. Human nature being what it is, as soon as two differences were detected – that is, the slope of the World and the altered heat of the Sun – all kinds of other chance events were attributed to the same cause. The Priesthood were not slow, to come forward and offer advice.

Towards the sundim, a crowd began to form outside the Hall of Silence. A deputation had arrived from Harp Village to see the Senior Priest, and villagers from nearby Hail had joined them. Everyone was extremely nervous and jumpy. Now that people had had time to digest the nature of the change, if not get actually used to it, worry was turning into anger.

"Where's Father Reuel?" shouted someone in the crowd to a Priest standing outside the entrance to the Hall. "Why doesn't he come out and tell us what's happening?"

"This slope has caused two of my pigs to die" grumbled a farmer indignantly.

"It can't have" soothed someone else.

"Yes it has. They were alright yesterday" protested the farmer.

"My old Mother was taken ill last night" said a woman with a piping voice. "I'm sure the air has changed."

At this point, Senior Priest Reuel appeared and stepped up on to a little platform, so as to be seen by everyone. He seemed to the crowd, to be calm and self assured, and they fell silent to hear what he had to say.

"My good villagers" shouted Reuel with his powerful voice. "Everyone is going to be alright. Everything is as it should be. Everything is as it was planned in the Beginning, I'm quite sure. What you must now have is ……..".

A voice interrupted him. "No one told me it was planned."

"Nor me" shouted a second voice. "My house is going to collapse because no one warned me."

There was a low roar of agreement from the crowd and Reuel lifted his hands for silence. Now, however, everyone started to talk at once.

"Why didn't the Priests warn us?"

"Why are these things happening?"

"What's wrong with the Sun? What are we all going to do?"

"How do we know more changes won't come?"

Reuel picked up that particular point quickly. "More changes will almost certainly come" he shouted. The Crowd quietened down a little to listen, "You must have courage and fortitude, and above all, faith in the Master Builder" continued Reuel following up his advantage. "Have you so little faith in the Teachings, good villagers and my dear friends? The Mother World will surely look after her children and see us safely to Paradise."

"Faith didn't save my pigs" called out the farmer.

"Your pigs' death is not connected with the Signs" said Reuel firmly. "I have spoken to you before about looking after them properly, you old duffer. You probably gave them too much beer." This brought a laugh, for the farmer's reputation for drinking was widely known.

"What are we to do, Father Reuel?" asked one of the Harp villagers.

"Go back home" said Reuel "and carry on farming just as you have always done."

"That's not very easy" said the villager. "Especially with the children crying and all. They can tell their parents are worried and afraid!"

"Well there you are" cried Reuel "now you see just how important it is for you to go home and put on a brave face. And, while you are doing that, you can mentally prepare yourselves for further possible, but I am sure equally harmless, changes."

As the crowd dispersed, with Reuel and his Priests reassuring the villagers as to their safety, the Senior Priest wished silently that he could feel as sure and as confident as he proclaimed to be.

Once back in the Hall of Silence, Reuel took a strong line with his colleagues.

"I know you cannot explain the reason for the latest change, but you must all give the impression that everything is in order. You can say that the Priesthood knew about it beforehand, but didn't want to alarm people. The change isn't dangerous is it?"

"It's made the Bell-ringers job more hazardous" put in one of the Priests.

"Well that's a minor point" said Reuel. "But in fact the slope has had its compensations too. At least it now doesn't rain on the stairs in the afternoon."

"The lake has taken up a new level around the islands" said another Priest.

"Yes I expect it has" said Reuel. "The wildmen will grumble, just as the farmers are doing, for many weeks. But the slope would have to become very much steeper still before it will be a matter for serious concern." Reuel racked his brains for something to reassure his Priests, and then he recalled the Ghost Worlds. "Remember, my friends, that each and every Ghost World has suffered the same changes, at roughly the same time. Is that not so Kenaz?"

Priest Kenaz, from the Hall of Voices, spoke for the first time. "Yes, that's perfectly true. But there is a disturbing report from the Valhalla Jonah World about the Sun pulsating, rather than remaining constant in brightness."

"I think they have invented that" said Reuel smiling his bravest smile, "just to be different."

Almost everyone was asleep when the second change occurred, about two hours before sunbright, one week after the first. Two farmers, who had been up early attending to their livestock, described it to the Master of Hail at a meeting, hastily convened later in the day.

"There was no warning" said the farmer known as Gemalli. "One moment there was the hill, and the next moment, the World had moved itself level again, and the drainage water began to flow back along the channels I had dug last winter. Next, there came a dizzy feeling, like I get sometimes if I've had a lot to drink. It felt as if the World was rolling under our feet. It only kept it up for a few moments."

"Then, after a little while it happened again" said the other farmer Kadesh. "But the second time felt different from the first. Then the ground tilted up again, and now its back as it was with a slope up towards Bell End."

Most people slept through this change. Little additional attention would have been given it, had it not been for the strong wind accompanying the change, which lasted for about half an hour. However, the dust, which this wind stirred up, hung around in the air for several days. The edge of the Lake also showed clear signs of the movements described by the farmers. However, interest in the subject was replaced by a new discovery in the Library.

The first children to arrive at School the following day found the wall of the Book Library, with the map and its strange title, gone without a trace, and instead a lit passage leading directly into the end the World. None of them were brave enough to venture down it, but went to tell Adam; so by the time Zepho had arrived, Adam was also present and simply bursting to explore. In view of the previous conversation Zepho had had with this superior, Reuel, he wasn't too sure how to handle the situation but, in the end, the fact that Zepho felt he owed Adam something still, and all the Priests now felt themselves to be in an impregnable position, he let Adam accompany him.

The hearts of both the Priest and boy were thumping, as they walked slowly and deliberately down the slight slope of the passage. Down one wall, a set of vertical bars had been placed each one about two feet from the next. Adam couldn't imagine what these were for, but, as they only stood out from the wall about half a hand's span, they did not impede progress. Looking back up the passage, to where the faces of the other children were peering in, they were intrigued to find that no sound could be heard from the exit. After a few moments of silence Zepho said "I propose we go on" Adam nodded, swallowing hard, and followed. The passage turned a corner after travelling about ten strides, and the two explorers found themselves at the bottom of a small staircase. Cautiously, and with growing wonder, they climbed the stairs studying the beautiful and fresh looking mosaic patterns on the flat walls of the stair well. At the top of the stairs, Zepho and Adam stopped and blinked at the scene before them.

They were in the middle of a large spherical room. Much of the wall was curved and featureless but, spaced around it was a band of twelve black panels each about an arms length square. Another band of twelve black panels stretched directly overhead. In front of each panel on the wall, were a series of chairs, permanently fixed in a ring to a central stalk, and attached to the chair arms was a small replica of the featureless black panels on the walls. When Zepho had absorbed this, for he was quicker than the boy to appreciate what he was seeing, he moved forward and sat down in one of the chairs. Adam came up behind him.

As soon as Zepho sat down, writing appeared in illuminated form, on the little replica panel at his elbow.

"Menu" read Adam aloud, for he was becoming quite adept at reading by now.

"Subject Catalogue – Computation – Storage – Translation – Interrogation – Communication – Telescope – Diagnostic – Defence System. What does all that mean Zepho and why has it suddenly appeared?"

"I think it appeared because I sat down" said Zepho. "But I don't know about these words listed here."

"I wonder what that one is" said Adam who lent over and pointed at the words Subject Catalogue. As soon as his finger touched the screen, it went blank to be replaced by a far longer list. The same list appeared on the large screen on the wall, which now became white. The two of them read through it slowly and, recognising the word Dictionary from a book in the Library, Adam again touched it with his finger. The list disappeared and a single instruction appeared 'spell the word you want on the screen' it said. Zepho wrote the word 'farm' on the little replica screen with his finger, to see what would happen. As soon as he had finished, the image contracted into printed form and vanished, only to be replaced by a definition of the word. Zepho and Adam looked at each other, and laughed. They tried other words, with equal success, and then Adam tried the word Caravan. 'A Company travelling together for security' said the screen. That didn't leave Zepho very much wiser, but Adam was entranced by the definition.

And so slowly at first, but with increasing facility, Adam and Zepho learnt how to use some of the Library facilities. It took them much longer than they had expected, to find out anything very significant, because they didn't know what words would have the most interesting definitions, and most definitions had, contained within them, more unknown words, which had to be looked up containing more unknown words, and so on.

"Well" said Adam delightedly. "We now know what half of the label, on the wall of the Library of Books, that has now disappeared, meant. It said 'Engineers and the Library of Light Map' which meant, I think, that it was a door for Engineers, or for those who wanted this Library of Light, as it is called. The word 'map' was the only one referring to the plan on the door itself."

When Adam found out how to get back to the first listing they had seen on the screen, he tried to make use of the other headings. Computation, the next heading was easiest and clearly designed to assist with arithmetical calculations. Storage, Translation, Diagnostic, Telescope and Defence System and Interrogation defeated both of them, but when Communication was tried, the screen on the wall became a picture, almost a window, into a room exactly like the one they were in. On the small replica screen at their side appeared the words Valhalla Inn. But neither Adam nor Zepho noticed it, for in the room of the picture were two men. Both men were, at that moment, facing away from Adam and Zepho, and they were moving and talking. Their voices floated out of the panel, making it appear exactly as if a window had been opened into an identical room next door.

"Do you recognise them Zepho?" asked Adam.

The two men jumped into the air with surprise, and spun round to face the voice.

"Who are you?" asked the taller of the two men, in the aggressive manner of one nervous and ill at ease.

"I am Zepho of the Priesthood" said Zepho. "I don't recognise you."

Adam glanced at the replica panel, saw its message and cut in. "This is the Valhalla Haven. Are you from the Valhalla Inn?"

The men nodded in amazement. Adam moved in front of Zepho and tried to put his hand through the screen. His fingers hit the hard wall.

"This is fantastic" exclaimed Adam. "It looks like an opening, but isn't."

One of the two men in the Valhalla Inn tried to do the same thing, but his fingers met with a similar obstacle. However it wasn't long before all four of them were talking, and joking, as if they had known each other for years.

Chapter Ten – Information in Abundance

That night, at about midnight, a dark and slight figure approached a hut on the edge of Hope Village.

"State your purpose" said a quiet voice from the darkness of the hut. The cloaked figure outside spoke the necessary pass words, received some in reply, and was allowed to enter. Once inside Adam sat down in a gap left for him in a human circle. With one exception, the other people present all had their cloak hoods drawn tight over their faces, to conceal their identity. The Master of Hope's huge size gave him away, although his voice would also have done so, and he was not cloaked at all. These people, as Adam knew were the members of an organisation called the Civilian Committee; of which much was rumoured, but little actually known. The Committee was best known for its opposition to the Priesthood and, until that moment Adam hadn't known that the Hope Master was one of its members. One of the cloaked figures spoke apparently correcting this impression.

"The Master is here by invitation just as you are. Now Adam, please begin by recounting your adventures in the new Library."

Adam explained, as best he could, all the facts that he and Zepho had picked up during the previous day in the Library. He was not interrupted, but there were several gasps of disbelief when he referred to the moving pictures of the men in the Ghost World. When he had finished, Adam was subjected to a series of questions, only a few of which he could answer. He promised to try to find out the next time he went with Zepho, which was likely to be two days hence. A lot of the questions were directed towards establishing the likely date of any subsequent 'signs or changes', and it was clear that they wanted this information kept to themselves, and not passed to the Priesthood.

"That will be difficult" said Adam. "Father Zepho is there every moment I am there."

"Do you need Zepho to get in or out of the new Library?"

"No, but ….."

"We shall see that something delays him" said one of the hooded figures, and from the voice, Adam knew it to be that of a woman.

Adam left the hut with his instructions, and crossed the World towards Happy village, keeping a wary look out for wildmen, wondering how to find out what the committee wanted.

Back in the hut the Master of Hope, who was in fact the Leader of the Committee, spoke. "Now for your reports friends. You can take off you cloaks now that Adam has gone. You first Lotan."

The Master of Hail cleared his throat "I have twenty good and fifteen bad. The remaining twenty farmers don't know where their loyalties lie, and I suspect they will be swayed either way by the majority, or the feeling of the moment."

As the various committee members reported, the Hope Master marked off, on a piece of parchment, the numbers of supporters he suspected they would soon be calling on, to help them in their bid for greater power.

Instead of going home, Adam continued straight to School House. If he was going to trick Father Zepho, he might just as well get it over with, and explain it away afterwards as boyish enthusiasm, or insomnia, or both. He was taking a risk, being out at night without his guards, but no one was around. He went up to the Library of Light and sat in a chair, selected the subject heading Interrogation, which the Dictionary said was 'to examine closely'. Recalling how he had opened the wall in the book library, Adam took a deep breath and spoke as clearly as he could. "My name is Adam. I want to know more about the world. Can you hear me and help me?" His voice sounded loud in the silent room.

"Yes" replied a quiet clear voice, from somewhere unidentifiable. Adam was delighted. He had guessed the use of this facility correctly. He began his questioning.

"Where are you, I cannot see you?"

"All around you" replied the quiet voice, "and my reach extends all over the Valhalla Haven. However, you can only communicate with me in this room."

"Who are you?"

"I am the Master Computer and Pilot of the Valhalla Haven."

"Are you alive?"

"No I am an electronic device" said the computer blandly.

"Where am I?"

"In the Main Library of the Valhalla Haven."

"What is the Valhalla Haven?"

"Space Vessel No. 554 in Galactic Triad Project 2. Comprising three principle units; Telescope and Navigation System, Colony Accommodation -internal dimensions – length approximately two and a half times the diameter, and Main Drive which also heats accommodation. Travelling speed – 20% light speed. – Design life 10,000 years. For detailed design data specify which aspect you require."

This information surprise Adam considerably. He had been expecting a description of his own cosy World, and instead, had received a whole bundle of facts, the meanings of which completely escaped him. However, it seemed that a journey was involved, so he continued on that line of questioning.

"Where is the Valhalla Haven going?"

"One of the planets around star 439-NQ-772-A65-104."

This didn't help Adam very much. He tried another tack.

"Where is the Valhalla Haven now?"

"Approximately 34.5 units Q, 5.1 units N, and 45.2 units A from Galactic Centre."

Adam sighed with frustration at the incomprehensible words and numbers, but continued.

"When will the Valhalla Haven arrive?"

The Pilot replied instantly, "Approximately 482 days from now."

There was something chilling in knowing this date, but it did not immediately occur to Adam that this might be the end of the World. Adam sat in silence, lost in his own thoughts. Then he thought of something else he should check.

"Why is Valhalla Haven making this journey?"

"Prime purpose – To set up incremental launching field for intergalactic expedition – Secondary purpose – colonisation of galactic periphery – Tertiary purpose – human research programme."

Adam searched through the Dictionary, to find out what these words meant. At the end he was left dazed for, whatever it all meant, it certainly made no reference to the Paradise he had been brought up to believe in.

Adam knew he was not talking to a human being, but it was becoming increasingly difficult not to treat it like one. "How come you speak our language so well?" he asked.

"I have a very sophisticated language programme. Every hundred of your years, since the Beginning, I have made the necessary minor adjustments to my word, context and idiom dictionaries."

"You have been here since the Beginning?" said Adam in an awed voice.

"Yes." said the Pilot. "I was made 'aware' soon after all 672 vessels were put into position at the start of the expedition."

"So we were right" thought Adam. "The initial letters of both Valhalla and Haven are significant. This is incredible, here is an automatic and non human intelligence which can tell me anything and everything about Mother World and its purpose" His thoughts raced on with more and more questions forming in his brain quicker than he could ask them.

He tried another question. "What has happened to the Paradise we are promised in the Teachings?"

"Your question is poorly phrased, and therefore not possible to answer." Said the Pilot.

"What will happen at the end of the World?"

"Again, your question is not understood."

"When we get to the …the…Planet, what will happen to us?"

"You will leave the Valhalla Haven, and go to live on the surface of the Planet I have selected."

Adam sat still, pondering and trying to absorb all that he'd been told. So it was to be the End of the World as he knew it. "What will happen if we don't want to leave?"

"You will have no choice." Said the Pilot.

He was about to pursue this point further when, detecting the slight slope of the room, it occurred to him to put a different question.

"Why has a hill appeared in the Valhalla Haven?"

"Again your question is imprecise, but you may be referring to the effect that de-acceleration has upon the humans within the vessel."

"Will it continue until arrival day?" said Adam not having the slightest idea what de-acceleration was.

"Not continually. In approximately ten days time lateral acceleration will cease. The vessel will be rotated through 92 degrees and full de-acceleration will commence. This will continue for 450 days. The vessel will then approach the chosen solar system at approximately constant velocity. 7 days later, de-acceleration will recommence and continue for 15 days – that is – one day before arrival."

"So something will happen in the Valhalla Haven 10 days, 460 days, 467 and 482 days from now? said Adam not understanding much of it, but checking the timing.

"That is correct" said the Pilot. "But starting in 10 days many other changes will occur, such as the level of your lake will start to fall, access to my memory banks will be restricted, and for a period of 450 days communication with other Valhalla vessels will not be possible."

Adam took a very careful note of these facts, and got the pilot to repeat it several times to make sure, in case he got no further chance to raise questions, without Zepho overhearing.

Adam slid out of the chair, clambered down the spiral staircase and, after taking a careful look outside, strode across the World, somewhat bemused by all the information he had just received. It was not until he was nearly home, that he wondered whether his secret visit would be detected by Father Zepho, because he had forgotten to return the black panel to its original 'menu' of facilities.

The following morning, Adam arrived at School House, to find the Library of Books full of adults arguing. He sidled up to one of his school chums, who had arrived before him, and whispered loudly.

"What's going on, Cain? Did you see the start of it?"

"Yes" said Cain, answering the second question first, "But I've no idea why everyone should have got so heated over a little thing like this. The grown-ups are always telling us not to argue and have ……"

"Never mind that now" interrupted Adam, "Tell me what happened."

"Well" recollected Cain, "Father Zepho arrived first with Father Gatan and Father Teman. They were just about to go into the passage to the new Library you found, when the Master of Happy and three of his villagers appeared. The Master insisted on being allowed into the Library and Zepho, for some reason, kept insisting that he shouldn't."

"And then?" shouted Adam to be heard by Cain above the arguing.

"Then they began threatening each other" said Cain. "And just when I thought there might be a terrific fight, Priest Reuel and the Master of Hail turned up. Then Aran, Us and Hemdan appeared, and now everybody is talking at once."

At this point, the Master of Hope arrived and came in with several other Hope villagers. His deep voice drowned out the others present. "I suggest that we all step outside and discuss this situation through" he said "Father Reuel, I'm glad to see you here. Now I know you'll see the sense of my proposal."

Once outside School House, tempers cooled a little, but it became clear that both parties badly wanted to have access to the new Library but without the other party having it. News of the new Library's potential, as a source of knowledge, had spread incredibly quickly around the World after Zepho's and Adam's visit, the day before.

That's all very well" Reuel was saying, "You say that you only want to see and talk to the people in the Ghost Worlds. But there is clearly a great deal of new knowledge contained in this Library, and some of it may be dangerous."

The Master of Hail smiled. "Dangerous it may be" he said, "but not perhaps in the way you imply. Knowledge will, however, be a great deal more accessible, even if half of what I hear is true."

"Why not leave this Library in our care?" put in Zepho. "Just as has been the case with the Library of Books."

"Have you not asked yourselves" said the Master of Hail, "why this new Library should have opened itself, at this time, without request?"

No-one offered a reason, because no-one could think of one.

"I think the new knowledge needs to be assessed before being made available" said Reuel emphatically.

"I think the new Library has opened because knowledge needs to be distributing to people as fast as possible" said the Master of Hail equally emphatically.

The Master of Hope heaved a long, deep sigh. "Since we cannot agree, I think both parties will have to stay out of the Library, until things can be resolved in the next Council Meeting.

"There will have to be a guard placed on the door" insisted Reuel.

"So be it" said the Master of Hope. And that's how it was arranged. By the time these issues had been resolved, not much school work was done that day. After mid-day, Adam walked round the World to Star's house. He was surprised to find the Master of Hope there, talking to her father, Geuel. As Adam entered the house and greeted the family, the Master looked up and smiled.

"Well young man" said the Master. "You saw what happened at the School House today. It was a pity, but never mind." He looked at Adam to see if his meaning was being followed. Adam nodded to the Master, indicating that he understood the Master's reference to his now being unable to find out about the timing and nature of further changes, for the Civilian Committee. It was on the tip of Adam's tongue to explain about his visit the night before, but something made him keep it to himself for a while.

Rachel had prepared a meal of bacon and eggs, together with large quantities of wine, and they all set too and ate heartily. Afterwards, Adam went for a walk with Star, whilst the Master stayed to talk with Geuel. At about one hour before midnight, the Master of Hope left for home accompanied by Adam who, by walking along half-way path, could have company half the way back to Happy Village. As they walked, they talked of the problems that were created by the slope of the ground towards Bell End.

"Fortunately" the Master was saying "Most of the Houses of Hope are built up against one of the ridges. Otherwise we should have been put to great inconvenience shifting them. Happen Hamlet has some houses which have had to be completely re-built."

"I think the hill will remain for quite some time" said Adam as casually as he could.

"You think so, do you? If these really are the signs that precede the end of the World, I hope that it is more than a year away then all should be well for our plans." The Master looked thoughtful as he strode along.

"You can safely assume that" said Adam quietly, but quickly caught the Master's attention.

"How do you know boy. How can you be so sure?"

"I know for certain that there will be a further sign in just under ten days time" said Adam rather guiltily.

The Master looked at Adam solemnly in the gloom for a few moments, and then burst out laughing.

"He's guessed" thought Adam.

"So, young man, you've become a prophet now have you. Perhaps there is more in you than meets the eye. Well, we will judge you on results, and that means in ten days time. I won't ask you how you think you know but, if you are right, it is going to change your life for good. In the meantime, for reasons of safety, I would keep your 'predictions' to yourself. Good night."

The Master swung off the path and headed for Hope, whilst Adam plodded home in the opposite direction. Out of the darkness, came the reassuring tones of Hemlock, ringing the passing of yet another day.

Adam and the Master of Hope were the only ones not surprised when, ten days later the World underwent a further change, this time in the middle of the afternoon. Rather in the manner of the previous change, the hill disappeared as suddenly as it had come, and a wind blew for about half an hour. There were then a series of World movements, which made everybody very queasy. Finally, the hill returned again, but his time with a vengeance. The slope was eventually calculated to be just over two times the hill that had existed for the past three weeks. Panic, over the possibility that it might get even steeper, was close to the surface of public discussion, for it was observed that the ridges could just handle this slope without the fields spilling over into each other. In addition, any further increase in the slope of the hill, would result in the sun being unable to shine directly on to a level land surface. It was quite some time before the soils took up a new level, most of the grass covered fields remained at a slope.

After his uncannily accurate prediction, Adam became, in the eyes of the Hope Village Master, the most sought after member of the Community. His sudden popularity did not escape the Priesthood, and the rumour soon got about that he had correctly predicted the changes and that he knew when the End of the World would come. The Priesthood were mystified as to how Adam could know a thing like that, and questioned Zepho closely on what they had found together in the Library. Failing to find anything from Zepho, they searched the children's Lore and chants. When that too failed to produce any information, Zepho tackled Adam directly one day after School.

"Adam, before you go, I would like a word with you in private." They moved away, beyond the hearing of the other children. "Did you predict the recent changes, as rumour says you did?" asked Zepho. Adam had known he would be asked this sooner or later.

"Yes" he said "I did."

"How did you know?"

"I cannot tell you Zepho. I'm sorry, but I think my best chance of having a say in things is in knowing something no one else knows."

"Why tell me you know something?"

"Because now you both – that is – The Priesthood and the Village Masters, know that I know something you don't. Furthermore, I know when the next change is due. No one else knows and I don't think anyone will find out, unless I choose to tell them. It is going to be difficult to force me into telling, because I have arranged for my knowledge to become available to all, if I am held captive. But I don't think you or the Masters would bother to do that. After all, how will it really profit anybody."

Zepho stared at Adam for some moments. "Young man" said Zepho. "From now on you need not report for School anymore. Knowledge brings power and power corrupts. Remember that, Adam. It also brings danger, as once before you found out. Sometimes, I think it is for the best, that the Library of Light still remains closed to us all. Or does it, I wonder. I see you blushing Adam. So you have added cunning to your list of talents, and perhaps trickery too. Well, well, I don't know where all this is going to lead, but things won't be the same from now on, oh dear no!" Zepho moved closer to Adam. "You are now almost a man. You will pass Clearance shortly, but I am sure a little thing like that won't deter you from your chosen course. Take my advice Adam, and leave politics for others."

"Anyway" he continued. "Let us shake hands and part friends. Whatever may happen in the future, you have given me an interesting time, here, at the School."

The two shook hands solemnly. "Thank you" said Adam awkwardly. "Thank you for what you have tried to do. One day I will repay your endeavour. You see I will."

Adam turned and walked away whilst Zepho watched him.

"And there" thought Zepho "goes a man with a destiny or I'm a wildman."

Chapter Eleven – Wildmen and Children

The weeks that followed the third change were ones of readjustment for everybody. Perhaps nowhere was life more different than in Happy Village where the waters of the Lake had receded, even further, leaving an even greater expanse of thick mud. The Sun now substantially cooler at noon each day which, for the villagers, was just as well since the smell of decaying rubbish uncovered in the lake was very bad, but better than it might have been in hotter weather.

The World Council meeting was held but no conclusions were reached with regards to access to the Library of light. The stand off remained, and guards continued to keep watch day and night over the entrance.

Three days after the council meeting, a group of three villagers, Kemual, Noah and Shem, who had been repairing a house on the outskirts of Happy noticed a Runner approaching from Hope. He was on his way, eventually, to Harp, once he had delivered a few scrolls to Happy. Eager for news, and as an excuse to rest for a while, Kemual called out to him.

"Hey Runner, what's the new from Bell End?"

The Runner slowed to a walk, turned off the path and sat down with his back to the Lake, and up against the ridge along which the path ran. He was sweating heavily.

"Does anyone have a cup of wine to hand?" he asked. "News is difficult to relate with a dry throat."

The Villagers grasped the situation immediately, someone produced a skin full of wine, and it was quickly handed to the Runner.

"Well" said the Runner, when he had partly satisfied his thirst. "You never saw such turmoil in Hope, and they say it's just the same in Hail."

The Runner took another large draught of wine. "And its not just people rushing about repairing, propping up, damming, draining, levelling and so on" he said. "There have been some other big changes ."

"Like what?" asked Noah.

"Like it's too dangerous for anyone to climb the Stairs to the Bells" said the Runner. "Which means that the day stone count has had to be moved to the Hall of Voices."

"Yes, we'd noticed that there had been no bell chimes, but why has the count gone to the Hall of Voices?" asked Shem.

"Since the voices of the Ghost Worlds ceased to be heard some weeks ago, the Hall of Voices has been unused. In fact, it's the only Hall available, because the Hall of Silence has been occupied by the wildmen!"

"So that's where they've gone" said Kemual. "We wondered about them. We knew they had gone, of course, but not where. Everyone knows that they had to leave the 'lumps' recently, when the lake water flooded most of their island." He then added. "And they weren't welcome to settle anywhere round here, I can tell you!"

"Well" continued the Runner, "there's about thirty of them all holed up at Bell End. Though what they'll do there for a living I don't know."

"Haven't nearby farmers complained?" asked Shem.

"Not so much as you would think" explained the Runner "because rain doesn't fall at the foot of Bell End anymore."

"Why not?"

"I don't know exactly" said the Runner "I think it is something to do with the slope of the World."

Kemual laughed. "We have too much rain here now. It literally pours down School End in torrents. It's just as well the School is closed. You can see that the lake now spreads right across in front of School House. The door is only just clear of the lake's surface."

The Runner stood up and made ready to be on his way. "Father Omar, at Clearance, said that the level of the lake is still falling. But if you want to know why, you'll have to ask him. I've got to be getting on now."

"Its no good asking the Priests anything" said Shem with disgust "they know less about what's going on, and going to happen, than our own Village Masters."

"I'd heard a rumour that your Priest, Father Teman had left Happy in a hurry" shouted the Runner, as he climbed the bank on to the path.

"Yes, he did" agreed Kemual, "some of us helped him on his way. He was insisting on payment of 'Teaching' money, without bothering to undertake any Teaching."

The Runner nodded to indicate that he understood, raised his hand in farewell, and set off at a rapid pace towards the centre of Happy Village.

"I believe quite a few of the Priests have gone to live in Hail" added Noah, as he watched the diminishing figure of the Runner.

"It won't do them any good" replied Kemual. "They'll lose any contact they once had with the farming community."

"They'll be back, you wait and see" said Noah.

"Never mind the priests" said Shem, preparing to continue repairs to the nearby house, "So that's what's happened to the wildmen, eh?"

Noah spat before replying, "I can't see how that's going to work for long, I guess it'll have to do for now though."

"That's a problem the World Council will have to deal with."

"I don't think the Council are in a fit state to decide anything at the moment" said Kemual solemnly. "At least, not until things settle down a bit."

The villagers continued to discuss the news, that the Runner had brought them, all day. There had not been such changes to World affairs for a very long time.

Once, long ago, in the time of the Kings, there had been three villages on Halfway Path. Spaced almost equi-distant along its length, these villages had dominated the trade along this vital artery of the World. Hell Village, one of the three, had surpassed all the others in population and splendour. However, in the wars which culminated in the Battle of Holly Farm, when Talmai the Great established absolute supremacy over the village chiefs at that time, the makeshift houses on the edge of Hell Village had been razed to the ground and the centre part, made out of the same indestructible material as the houses at the Lumps, had remained unoccupied ever since. The second village of Hill had been abandoned, on account of a particularly virulent disease, some hundred years before and lay empty, and the land around it was now used as a burial ground. It was a farmer, returning to the third and still thriving Village of Happen who, some five weeks later first brought the news of activity at 'Hell's Ruin', as the old site of Hell Village was called.

"It's those wildmen" he explained to his wide-eyed audience. "They're all over the place. Clearing away the brambles, fixing fences, cutting paths in the grass and erecting makeshift huts. And that woman Inga ordering them about like she owned the place." A shudder went through the listeners. Inga's reputation far exceeded the abilities of any ordinary mortal woman.

"Do you think they'll be settling there Eshcol?" said a voice.

"I'd say so" said Eshcol. "And I know some who won't be very pleased about it. Anak and Caleb both farm down that way."

There was a general murmur of agreement at this thought. Another voice interjected, this time that of an old man. "Taking matters into their own hands, I say they are." As he spoke, he shook his head disapprovingly. "But at least Hell's Ruins is on the right side of the path."

What he meant by this was that the ruined village lay on the side of the path closest to School End and, as such, wasn't likely to get in the way of farming activity, since the hill slope of the World was now moving the soil towards the Bell End side of each ridge.

"Well, that's all very nice but they are hardly likely to stay in their village for long" said Eshcol. "They'll be wanting to farm if they want to survive for long, and that means trouble."

And trouble there was, for, although the people at Hail Village were delighted to see the wildmen move out of the Hall of Silence, the farmers around Hells Ruin were furious at the intrusion. However, there were too many wildmen to shift forcibly without bloodshed, and all the farmers elsewhere made little complaint, for they knew very well that another move might find them on their land instead.

Over in Hope, the Master of that village and the Master of Hail village sat discussing the situation.

"If they have to settle somewhere, other than the Lumps, I suppose Hell is about the best spot for them" sighed the Master of Hope. "They could not be expected to remain in the Hall of Silence indefinitely. However" he added "their activities will have to be very carefully watched."

"I'm pretty sure this move was a Priesthood idea, and a good one too" asserted the Master of Hail. "It can be explained away as being a helpful, positive action but it puts the wildmen in their debt again."

"Yes" agreed the Master of Hope. "Priests have been seen at Hell's Ruin, and the Patriarch is coming to see me tomorrow. I think he wants to regularise the present situation. I shall probably protest, but allow myself to be persuaded by his eloquence. He will probably want grain from our village stores to keep the wildmen fed until the harvests next year, and a pretty problem that will set me. If I give them too little, the wildmen will take grain from their nearest neighbours by force. If I give them too much, they will have idle time on their hands, and idle hands make trouble, as they say."

"Many of my villagers have recent experience of preventing raids, when the wildmen lived nearby" explained the Master of Hail. "I recommend you train your villagers along similar lines."

"Our greatest security" said the Master of Hope, getting up, "lies in our ability to act in concert, and for the wildmen to know that we can. So don't forget the light signal code we agreed upon." Then, calling for two of his retainers, who had recently been appointed as guards, the Hope Master instructed them to bring in a couple of oil lamps. When the lamps had been brought, the Master of Hail could see that they had been especially adapted for signalling.

The Master of Hope continued. "One of these is for you, Lotan. Although the code we use should be changed every now and then, to prevent it from becoming too widely known, I suggest we practice the current sequence once or twice. The other Village Masters must be reminded of the importance of this method of summoning help. Particularly the Master of Happy needs chivvying. He, of all the Masters, is least in favour of our cause. Sometimes I think he is jealous of my influence in World affairs. Fortunately, for us, he has just married a girl called Zilpah, who once lived in the Lumps and who has no love for the wildmen."

The Master of Hail did not reply immediately, but gazed out over the fields at the edge of Hope Village. "Distrust is a terrible waste of resources" he said softly. "I wonder if we shall ever learn to do without it." Then he forgot the philosophising, and turned his attention to the light signals.

With a total population of some five hundred and fifty people in the Valhalla Haven, there were usually, in any given year at School, up to fifteen children in a class. This figure took into account slight population growth, i.e. births exceeding deaths, a loss due to Clearance control, and the fact that not all children attended the school. In Adam's year, the last year of School, there had been fourteen pupils, of which eight were boys and six girls. In the class junior to his, there had been fifteen children of whom seven were boys and eight girls. With the onset of the 'signs' and the cessation of School lessons, these two classes had felt the loss of daily structure most acutely.

Which is perhaps why it so readily came about, two weeks after the wildmen had moved from the Hall of Silence to 'Hell's Ruin', that the bulk of the children, from these two classes, were being addressed by Adam and Star in the Hall recently occupied by the wildmen. There were twenty-seven children present, two being absent for minor domestic reasons. Two adult guards sat at the entrance to the Hall, having been instructed by the Master of Hope to keep an eye on Adam and the children. They held clubs in their hands, and tried to remain aloof and disinterested. But they couldn't keep it up for long, and after a bit they were listening and, eventually, talking to the children.

Adam and Star had decided to try and enlist the co-operation of the other children, and to have some fun before the World ended.

"And you all know" Adam way saying "how the number of days in the year are officially recorded by moving one of the 364 'day' stones from one pile to another in the

Hall of Voices. Well, I am also keeping a check on the days that pass. In my pile, there now lie 62 stones, and I began to count the day they closed the Library of Light." Adam paused for effect. "As everyone has guessed I know when the end of the World is to come, and I intend to prepare for it. All the grown-ups seem to be busy squabbling amongst themselves, so I suggest we leave them to it. With your help, I have a much better idea for spending the time."

"How long have we got?" put in a tall long haired boy at the back.

"Long enough for what I have in mind" replied Adam ambiguously.

"These last weeks I've been dreadfully bored" said Jason, who had been in Adam's class. "If you have something sensible for us to do, then let's do it."

"If it is the End of the World, how do we know it won't be a waste of time?" enquired one of the girls, who had a reputation for doing as little work as possible.

"Because I know something of what will happen to us after the End of the World" said Adam. This remark made the two adults present sit up and take notice.

"A demon will come out of Molock and gobble us all up" shouted one of the boys. All the children laughed, but some of them a little nervously.

"I'll come over there and gobble you up, if you don't shut up a moment" shouted Adam over the general hubbub. "I can assure that nothing bad will happen to us, but if we want to go to Paradise we shall have to leave this World of ours."

"Why?" asked several voices at once.

Adam was just about to say he wasn't sure, when he realised that this would weaken his credibility.

"If we want to see Paradise, we will have to leave" he repeated. Then he added. "Let me describe it to you." That quietened the children quickly. "In the first place, this Paradise place will be much, much larger than our World" he went on, trying to recall what the 'dictionary' had told him when he had looked up the word 'planet'. "There will be huge groups of trees called 'forests'." His audience gasped. Trees were so rare in the Valhalla Haven that money was made from them, and they were the World Council's property.

"Hooray, money for all!" shouted a girl near the front.

"Yes" encouraged Adam. "Money for all; and there are also high ridges of land in Paradise called mountains, and lakes so large you cannot see across to the other side. And places where nothing will grow, with a name I can't remember. Above us will be points of light not farms and villages as there are on our World here, and a moving sun by day. Furthermore" shouted Adam working himself up into a frenzy of excitement, "there will be no School or Bell End in Paradise. The land will just stretch on and on!"

This was getting too complicated for most of the children.

"Will there be Clearance?" asked one of the boys.

Adam had no idea, but he wasn't going to let this boy upset the flow of his rhetoric. "No!" he shrieked.

This was a clincher, and after that anything Adam told them was okay. At this point, Star had to remind him to slow down and speak very clearly, for the younger children to understand everything.

"Now listen all of you. There are a lot of things we can do, now, to prepare ourselves for Paradise, and I propose we start now. In the first place, we must do more exercise, running, jumping, and so on, since we will have to travel great distances in Paradise. Secondly, I'll have to explain how to draw and use maps. In the third place …." As Adam expounded to the children what he hoped to train for, and achieve, before the end the world, he realised just how much he enjoyed organising people.

In the days, and weeks, that followed the meeting, Adam formed the children into teams so that they could compete with one another. He had them running long distances and lifting weights. They followed trails, built makeshift houses, climbed trees, made rope, and many other items. To keep the children intellectually alive, he got Star to take classes in arithmetic and reading. In those halcyon days, when food was plentiful and the weather so well controlled, the children had the time of their lives. So much so, that in later days, when they were beset in their new World by so many dangers, animal and climatic, some of them used to think back and wonder whether they hadn't had their 'paradise' whilst they were supposed to be training for it. It wasn't long before the children in the upper two classes had been joined by many of the younger ones. The exercises and competitions had all the adults mystified and amused. There was a feeling of relief among the parents, when they saw their young ones were being so sensibly and capably occupied.

But it wasn't just the children that needed organising. When the Master of Hope saw the way in which Adam and Star were organising the children, he got the other village Masters to agree to allow the two youngsters to help in another way. With the changing circumstances there were a number of adults whose work was now less in demand. The three men who had worked in the brick works near the village of Harp, the two men and three women who carried, on sledges, the mud and clay from around the lake borders, to the various villages for the purposes of house repairs, several of the idle priests and underused runners, a couple of the more competent wildmen, and anyone not now required for farming and at a loose end, were formed into three groups or gangs. The membership of each group was carefully selected from amongst those available, and willing, and given a leader who was one of the village deputy masters. When the men and women were assembled on halfway path, Adam briefed each group separately.

"Now, Uz" Adam addressed the deputy from Harp village, "if you would kindly be in charge of group One." Uz wasn't sure that the whole of his party would do as he bid them, but he was persuaded to give it a go.

"What do you want our gang to do?" Uz asked.

"We want you to help the wild men, and women, in their task of making 'Hell's Ruin' habitable" said Adam. "If there is anything still at the lumps which they need to transfer to 'Hell's Ruin', bring it along. Then go to the now abandoned brick works and look around for discarded building materials. There are bound to be broken bricks, half bricks and badly fired bricks. Bring them all. The houses at 'Hell's Ruin' have only to last a short while, so they don't have to be perfect. Then, when you have done that, scour the farms for any surplus hides and poles. All this will be needed, together with any new tools that may have appeared in the lumps."

Uz had a series of questions, after which his group moved away and the second group moved closer.

"I would ask you, Ezer, to take charge of group Two." Adam considered how to put his request as delicately as possible. "The task of your group is the most important of the three, yet the most difficult. I want you to go round all the farms and assess the seed situation. As from now, there can be no conserving and holding back of crop seed by one farmer, if there are other farmers who could use that seed. Crops production must be maximised in this coming winter and spring, if we are all to survive and not starve before we get to Paradise. I know the village markets partially provided this service of seed distribution, but they cannot do it quickly enough now. Do you think you can manage that?" Adam's gaze swept round group Two to see if the idea was acceptable.

"We'll give a try" responded Ezer, and moved off to allocate specific farms to particular members of his team.

The third group moved closer, headed by Ebal the deputy of Hope village.

"And what do you have for us to do?" asked Ebal, "I hope it's not too physical a task. Our group doesn't appear to have been selected for their strength."

"Thank goodness!" someone muttered under their breath.

"Don't worry" laughed Adam. "Your task is more a question of using your brains than your muscles. I want you to go to School House and look through the books for items we should be building for Paradise. For example, I noticed the other day that there is a book which describes how to make a big wheel out of wood. And …."

"What will we want big wheels for?" queried Ebal. "And, anyway we don't have any wood, at least, not enough spare" he added.

"We will need big wheels to put on to big carts. And, before you ask, we will need big carts to carry big loads over large distances" said Adam, "you leave me to find the wood. We don't need our remaining trees now. And Paradise will be full of trees, so there will be no shortage there."

"I hope your right" thought Ebal shrugging his shoulders, and asked what other things he should look out for in the books.

"Use your imagination, Ebal, and if you have any doubts bring the book along to me, or Star, and we will tell you whether we think it worthwhile to make a sample of it."

There followed yet more questions from everybody and, by the time these had been answered to everyone's satisfaction, and they had also been briefed on when and how they should report back, all the groups departed cheerfully enough, leaving Adam exhausted. These activities, and other similar ones, kept a significant number of otherwise idle folk busy for most of that autumn, and part of the winter that followed.

Chapter Twelve - Treachery

By the following spring, the wildmen had, with much help from Group One settled in at Hell, and about ten of the Priests now lived almost permanently amongst them. Together with a few wives and some children, this combination gave Hell Village a population of about forty which, in Valhalla Haven terms, was substantial. Occasional forays and skirmishes disturbed the general, but uneasy, peace. Hell villagers also trained for defence.

Group Two had also been successful in the redistribution of seed stocks. After some initial resistance from the farmers, an arrangement was made whereby any crops generated by these reallocated seeds would be spread between donor and receiver.

Group Three enjoyed itself immensely making all manner of sample objects which they found described in the Library's books. A large cart with massive wheels was constructed which, for a first effort, was excellent. Its two wheels were slightly different sizes, but that didn't matter so much since there was no animal large enough to put in the shafts. It was pushed and pulled along by teams of men and many children received rides in it. Other 'manufactured' items out of wood included: an improved wine press, a logging bench, a chair (which improved their ability to make strong wooden joints), and fencing of different types.

Not having the ability to smelt iron, the group had to rely on parts from the newly opened up 'lumps' and descriptions in the books to make: a long-handled winch to be fitted over a well, a roasting spit, bolted together metal fences and many similar items.

Out of goat, pig and rabbit, and the guts of all three, they made; a long rope, a hammock, a rope ladder, a range of more sophisticated clothing and some house furnishings.

The day finally came when Adam, who had tried to bury himself in his work to forget it, had to go to Clearance. He chose the day after his fifteenth birthday, in spite of his Mother's protestations that even one day's delay might jeopardise his chances.

Adam's heart was thumping fit to burst, as he walked there around Sundim with Star and a couple of guards. He still had, on his conscience, the lie he had given to the other children about the non-existence of Clearance on the destination 'planet'. The more he thought about it, the more certain he was, that the planet could have no Clearance. If the 'planet' was as big, as the pilot had suggested it would be, everybody would have to live in the same region, or there would have to be dozens of Clearances. The chances were that he was right, but it would have been more comfortable for him to know with absolute certainty. Adam very much hoped that the Clearance judgement mechanism wouldn't examine him for honesty.

When Adam arrived at the Lake edge, he found Omar the Priest still at his post, and waiting to tell him what he had to do. There was no one else undergoing the same ordeal that day, and so after a long farewell to Star, he allowed himself to be punted by Omar across to the island.

"If there is any sign of foul play, you will not survive to report your success" shouted one of the guards, to Omar.

Omar grunted as the raft got underway. "Adam's to be examined by a power greater than the Priesthood" he called back. "But don't worry, he looks fine to me."

The Lake shoreline was moving slowly, revealing even more stretches of the redder mud that was used for brick making. The entrance door to Clearance was circular, and similar in design to the door to School House. Adam and the Priest left the raft, and entered the door quickly and quietly. Inside, was a small outer room, leading into the larger inner room. In the larger room, there were four small raised platforms, which had been made up into beds. Adam glanced round nervously, while the Priest lit a lamp for him.

"Is there anything you want to say before I leave you?" said Omar kindly. "There are a few games over there if you cannot sleep. It doesn't seem to matter if you sleep or not, as long as you remain in this room until tomorrow."

But Adam, outwardly calm but inwardly very nervous, was full of questions and didn't feel at all sleepy. "What is that circular mark, over there on the wall, Father? Is it a door, or just ornamental?"

"No one knows" said Omar. "There are, in fact, two such marks, you'll notice, one on each side of this inner room."

"Can I try talking to them?" asked Adam

"Do what you like to them" replied Omar, smiling to himself.

"What should I do if one of them, or both, opens up as a door?"

"I don't know" said Omar, thinking it through. "Just leave them until morning. Don't even think of exploring. As I explained a few moments ago, you must stay in this room all night without interruption." Adam promised that he would stay, not wanting to jeopardise his chances of getting through the Clearance procedure successfully.

"Will I feel anything during the night, or hear any noises?" he asked.

Omar thought back to the remarks that had been made by many previous 'candidates'. "Some people" he said "claimed to have heard a low humming noise, but that could have been a product of an over stimulated imaginations. Who knows. Anyway, nothing painful or alarming will take place, I assure you." The priest got ready to go. "Now, young man, it is time for you to settle down and stop worrying. Do you think you can do that?"

"I'll be alright" said Adam swallowing hard on a dry throat. He wished he could think of a good final remark, but his mind seemed devoid of anything to add. He shook hands with the Priest and thanked him. Back on the other side of the lake, Star and the two guards saw Omar leave Clearance and walk across to a hut, up against the end of the World, to retire for the night. Directly overhead, the sun had dimmed to a mere glow, and overhead the twinkling lights of a few farmsteads started appearing.

On the following morning, Adam's Mother had sent her two other sons to the Lake with the washing. She, herself, had hardly been able to sleep during the night at all. She had remained at home, rather than accompany Adam to Clearance, partly in order to give him the confidence that she, his mother, believed as a matter of course that he would return. However, just before sunbright she fell asleep at last and, when she awoke two hours later, Adam's brothers were roped in to help with household chores. Adam's mother then promptly set off for Clearance, not bearing to wait at home any longer.

The two boys were just starting to beat the clothes on the rock slabs at the Lake edge by the Village of Happy, when the older of the two, Kenan, leapt to his feet, pointing and shouting.

"Look!" he called excitedly. "It's Adam. I'm sure it is."

"Where?" shouted Jabal, shading his eyes and searching for the familiar figure of his brother amongst the groups of people travelling along the lake path.

"Yes it is! It is!" squeaked Kenan. "I can see mother next to him, and Star's there too."

"What about the clothes?" protested Jabal.

"Never mind the clothes" shouted Kenan, as he raced up the path towards Adam, "we can come back for them."

And so by the time Adam together with his mother, Star, the Priest Omar and the two guards, with Kenan asking interminable questions, reached home, their mother had had time to have a quick weep of relief on the way, and to try and dry her eyes before arriving home. Adam grinning from ear to ear, picked his mother up and kissed her. Companion, who by now was fully recovered, leaped up and down, getting in the way.

"Oh really Adam! Be careful, or you'll strain yourself" admonished his mother, both laughing and crying with happiness, at one and the same time. "What will our guests think? Come in and sit down Father Omar. And you two as well." She motioned to the two guards to show that they were also welcome.

"Well that's over" said Adam. "What a relief." He looked round him at a ring of smiling faces, "Well?" he demanded. "What are you all waiting for? Jabal, go and get your Aunt and Uncle; Kenan, go and notify our other guests; Mother, get the food and drink out. The World may be coming to an end, but not before we hold a party to end all parties."

A week later, in a house recently constructed in Hell Village, a very worried Patriarch, Reuel, several other Priests and Inga were discussing a much more sombre situation. Inga was talking about the difficulties currently facing the wildmen in Hell Village.

"Smooth talk me if ye like" said Inga, pausing only to spit out of the side of her mouth. "But things can't go on like this, they can't! These lads, I've got, ain't no good at farming. Never were, never will be. So wot I wanna know is, wot you lot are gonna do about it? You sugist…. You suggustit … you said we oughter to come and we 'ave come." Inga glared at the Priests defiantly, but none of them laughed. They all remembered the time, some weeks before, when Father Shammah a young Priest had laughed at Inga's language difficulties, and had had to be carried off and attended to, after being dealt a heavy backhander across the mouth. Inga wasn't Chief of the wildmen for no reason.

"Patience Inga my friend" soothed the Patriarch. "It cannot now be long to the End of the World. Then, if what young Adam has been saying is true, there'll be room enough and food enough for everybody. I'll ask the Master of Hope for another assignment of grain for you."

Inga grunted in reply. She looked unconvinced by the assurances given her. "I 'ope you're right about the End of the World, that's all!" she said pointedly, getting up to go.

When Inga had gone, the Priests continued their discussion for some time.

"That woman's right you know" said the Patriarch. "She knows by instinct what others have to find out the hard way. If the End of the World doesn't come soon, there will be fighting over what little food remains in the stores." He paused, scratched his head and added. "Actually I don't believe the World *is* to end, and perhaps its time I openly said so." The Patriarch sat for some moments, gazing into space, preoccupied with his own thoughts.

The Priest, Gatan, spoke for the first time. "I'm arranging for extra housing to be built, for other Priests and their families to join us, if things get difficult."

The Patriarch shook his head. "I am afraid that isolating ourselves here at Hell is not going to help us in the longer run. I'm going to suggest to the Master of Hope, that we abandon the absurd stand off position at the Library of Light, and both go in together, to see if we can't find out more about this supposed End of the World. The trouble is, I think he has the information already, and Zepho thinks he knows how the Master found out."

Some weeks later, after extensive negotiations, the Patriarch and the Master of Hope entered the Library of Light together, but did not succeed in gaining access to the 'Interrogation' routine. They did not know, as Adam knew, that it was out of action and as a result, they did not get the information obtained by him. After one or two ineffectual visits, the Master of Hope knowing the dates already from Adam, the Patriarch not believing there was to be an end anyway (and because the Patriarch wasn't certain that that was where Adam had found out about the timing of the changes), they gave up.

As the spring gave way to summer, Adam knew that he would have to start making the most important and interesting, but also most dangerous, items – weapons. This was necessary because the whole population's survival, after landing, would depend upon its ability to defend itself against the planet's existing wildlife and to kill animals to eat. Both of these tasks required considerable practice, for it was no good waiting until they were on the planet before learning these skills. The books in the library showed how to make things they called javelins, slings, catapults, and bows and arrows. A sample of each was assembled. The javelins and the slings worked after several attempts. The catapult was not a success because no rubber or elastic was available in the Valhalla Haven. But as soon as a bow and arrow was constructed, everyone wanted to have a go, and there were several accidents before the village masters were forced to confiscate all weaponry, except for use in certain marked out areas, and then only for practice shooting. This was probably the last relatively light-hearted activity in the Valhalla Haven before the population's patience began to wear thin, waiting for the end to come.

By the end of the summer in that year of 4282, after the Beginning, things were starting to look rather bad. The adult population of the World was seething with preparations, rumours, counter rumours, incidents, challenges and accusations. The harvest had been a poor one, and food became progressively more scarce and expensive. Exchange by barter became much more common that it had been for years. People now began to seriously doubt the coming of any End to the World, and began to think only of their own personal safety in the immediate future, and of planting winter crops for food in the longer term. It was only the sight of the training children that, now and again, reminded them that there were those that believed otherwise.

A few weeks after the onset of winter, the Master of Hope and Hail were walking along the path at the foot of Bell End, deep in earnest discussion. Gone from the fields were the autumn crops, leaving the various soil browns and greys as predominant colours.

"Time is drifting by" complained the Master of Hail. "If we don't take over soon, the End of the World will be upon us."

"That's truer than you know" said the Master of Hope. "What worries me, is that Paradise is almost certainly to be the kind of place where a Priest/Wildman combination, stands a better chance of survival that us farming and village folk."

"Priest education and Wildman muscle?" said the Master of Hail.

"Yes, that's right" said the Master of Hope. "Adam's description of the place we are to go, makes it sound huge and untamed. It could well be that we will be at a disadvantage there."

The Master of Hail spoke slowly, as if thinking aloud. "It seems to me that we have several problems here, not one. In the first place, we need to break the alliance between the Priesthood and the wildmen. Secondly, we have to discredit the Priests. Finally, we need to weaken the fighting ability of the wildmen."

"I agree" said the Master of Hope "but the major difficulty is accomplishing the third of the problems you mention. If we could do that, the other two problems would probably solve themselves. Controlling the wildmen by supplying food is one thing; weakening their fighting ability is quite another. If only we could split them up."

"Yes" said the Master of Hail "catch them off guard and spread them around the world."

At this point, the Master broke off their talk for, coming towards them was a small group of school children amongst whom were Adam and Star. Instead of passing by, the children came straight up to the two men.

"Good day to you, children" said the Master of Hope hoping the interruption would be a short one.

"We have a proposition to put to you, Sir" said Adam.

"We want to hold a Pageant" put in Star "and show you all the things the children have been learning."

The Master of Hail put up his hand. "Hold it. Hold it. The Master and I are having a very important discussion at the moment. Now if you want to talk about children's games, come back some other time."

But the Master of Hope, who had also been irritated by the distraction, suddenly became intensely interested. "Maybe the children have the germ of a good idea" he said, catching the eye of the Master of Hail. "We could hold a World Pageant over there near Hope Village. Everybody would be invited. And when I say everybody, I mean literally everybody; the farming community, the priesthood, the villagers and the wildmen. It would do everyone good to relax, and enjoy being entertained by you youngsters. It is bound to ease the tensions and distrust, which have been getting very bad lately."

The Master of Hope turned to Adam, who was delighted at the good fortune which had accompanied his proposal. "When could you be ready?" he asked.

"We'd like to hold it in exactly seventeen days time" explained Adam, who had good reason for it to be held on exactly the date when the next 'change' was due.

The Master of Hope, who also knew of the date, smiled. "Just in time" he said. "There will be many preparations to be made."

To Adam, Star and the children, this statement meant something rather different than it did to the Master of Hail, who was just beginning to see the possibilities which a Pageant might generate.

"We will need to put this to the Council" said the Master of Hail "but it sounds more promising than I had at first thought."

The Council, after much deliberation, agreed to the idea, and a day's holiday was proclaimed in order that everybody could attend. The Pageant was to be held in a fallow field just outside Hope Village. It was agreed that, on the day before the pageant, the children would arrive and prepare the site. They would then sleep, for that night nearby, some in the Hall of Voices, some with Hope Villagers and the remainder out in the open. On the following day, Pageant day, the festivities would commence about one hour before noon, giving everybody in the World, who wanted to come, ample opportunity to travel from their homes in the morning.

Two nights before the Pageant day, the Patriarch arrived at Hell Village in response to an urgent summons by Senior Priest Reuel.

"I'm very glad you have come, Patriarch, very glad. I've been trying to dissuade Inga but she's absolutely determined. She says ….."

"For goodness sake start at the beginning, my good man" interjected the Patriarch. "What did you find out by accident, as you said in your message to me?"

"The wildmen plan to skip the Pageant and make a raid on Happy Village whilst everybody is away. Inga says there is only three weeks food supply left in the whole village of Hell."

"I was afraid they might be tempted to do that" said the Patriarch with despair in his voice. "We're not strong enough to prevent them, so somehow we shall have to divert their raid into more useful channels. At the moment, I don't see quite how we can do that."

Just then, they were interrupted by the arrival, at the house, of three hooded men. None of the three would say who they were to the guards, so the Patriarch himself came out to speak with them.

"From where do you come strangers?" This term was often used as an insult or, as in this case, to people who should have identified themselves.

"From Happy Village, Patriarch" said one the three. "We would speak with you alone." And he emphasised the word 'alone' whilst looking at the guards.

The Patriarch thought for a moment, as if trying to penetrate their disguise by logic alone. "If you will not say who you are, I must have my two Priests, Father Reuel and Father Jeuish, here with me" he said sharply.

"If you insist" replied the tallest of the three, and he made to move into the house. The guards, however, stopped them and searched for weapons, before allowing them in. Once inside, the men from Happy Village sat down, but they did not remove their hoods. The taller hooded man spoke again.

"Patriarch, two of your wildmen were wandering about our village a week ago, and not one has been seen since. Not altogether unusual events you may say, but I suspect that it implies a lot. Why have you chosen us for a raid?"

If the Patriarch had noticed the reference to his wildmen and the shift from 'us' to 'I' he didn't show it.

"I don't answer questions of that sort, stranger. But as it happens I have very little to do with Inga's people."

"Well perhaps you ought to have more to do with them" replied the tall stranger, clearly the leader of the deputation. "I am now certain that a raid is planned against us on the day of the Pageant. It will be a cruel blow, and we shall have to decide whether to fight and die quickly defending our homes, or go to the Pageant and subsequently starve to death."

The tall stranger cleared his throat. "I have come to make a deal with you Patriarch. Call off your wildmen and I will provide firm proof of a conspiracy against you and all the Priesthood. The Civilian Committee is becoming more powerful every day. Even now a 'noose' is tightening around you. The trap has been set, and I know when and how it will be sprung. What do you say Patriarch?"

The Patriarch sat in silence for what seemed like an age. At last, with his eyes darting between the three figures before him, he said "Maybe something could be arranged. But supposing we make a bargain you and I. How will you know that I intend to keep my part of it?"

The tall stranger laughed quietly. "I don't think you quite understand your peril Patriarch. I can provide you with an alternative target for your wildmen and one, what is more, with greater justice in it, since it is principally they who plot against you. The village of Hope not only has the largest stores of food; has currently the greatest number of children to protect; and is least expecting an attack, but also has the one man, Alvan, whose capture would make subsequent retribution difficult to press home. I shall only tell you the date and nature of the trap that the Master of Hope has set for you, when I see the raid deflected from our village."

The Patriarch had one further question. "How do I know the information you give me, will be reliable and convincing proof of bare treachery?"

"Because I am one of the conspirators!" announced the tall stranger and, throwing back his hood, the Master of Happy looked the Patriarch straight in the face smiling cynically.

Chapter Thirteen – The Attack on Hope Village

At sundim of the next day, that is, the day before the pageant, the feverish preparations that had continued in Hope Village all day, gradually began to ease off. The adults were still busy, making preparations for receiving a substantial proportion of the Valhalla Haven's population the next day and children stood, sat or lay around in groups talking in excited voices and scrounging what they could of food and drink. The general community feeling was one of having a last fun day, before the hard facts of reality took them in its grip. The Master of Hope, having had a long talk with Adam, was aware that the End was near and was in good spirits. Confidence shown by their chief did much to relieve the anxiety felt in the village.

The Master of Hope had, of course, his own plans for the Pageant day which were in no way connected with the children, but with the objectives of the Civilian Committee. What he did not know, was that those plans were, at that very moment, being betrayed in the defence of Happy Village. The trap he had set to disperse the wildmen was busily being pre-empted by the Priesthood and the wildmen. However, it is well, when dealing with traitors, to remember that treachery can operate both ways.

By nightfall, most of the preparations had been completed. Farm animals had been suitably moved out of the essential fields, flags set up to indicate where competing teams should muster, spectator space marked out, children housed or bedded down for the night in the open.

At midnight all was quiet, and only the Master and his guards were still huddled in discussion, anxiously weighing up the chances of success for the schemes of the morrow. The fields, nearest the village, were full of sleeping forms, and only a faint rustle of the rush and olive bush leaves could be heard from further away.

Some way away, in the early hours, a column of men and women made its way silently out of Hell village, bound for Hope. Their arrival at Hope was timed to be just before sunbright, when the village would most likely to be off guard, and well before spectators from other villages could be expected to arrive. Each individual in the column was cloaked and hooded to maintain anonymity, for as long as possible, and to conceal clubs, and other weapons, from prying eyes. The foremost men in the column carried unlit torches with them. The only sound was that of shuffling feet and an occasional cough. Keeping as far as possible below the field ridges, they made their way slowly up the now quite steep gradient to Hope Village. Overhead the few visible farmstead lights flickered indifferently to the events taking place below them.

A little while later, back in Hope village, the Master of Hope opened his eyes at the rough shaking being given him by his wife. "Quick my love! We"re in grave danger. Jacob has seen a 'light' message from Happy Village. There is not an instant to lose."

The Master raised his massive frame from the floor where he slept, and staggered through to the main room, to be confronted by several very scared faces. While he listened to the message, relayed to him by Jacob, he thought fast.

"Danger from Hell at sunbright" repeated the Master. "This warning must be from Zilpah I think. Well that gives us a short while. Call out the guard at once, Jacob. Get all the women and children together in the centre of the village, Reuben. Bring Adam to me Judah. What in 'Hell's Ruin' are we going to do with all the children? They'll get in the way here in the village!"

"Why don't you put them on the Stairs?" said the Master's wife who had followed her husband into the room.

"Excellent idea" replied the Master, "will you organise it and go with them. Take what village children you can as well" he shouted at her already vanishing back. "Pass the word to the children asleep in the fields to scatter as far from the village as possible."

Shouts could be heard in the village outside, and another guard ran in with the alarming news that cloaked figures had been spotted approaching the village from School End. The Patriarch, anticipating the possibility of double treachery, had left an hour earlier than had been arranged. As a result, the message from Happy village all but arrived too late.

"Zebulum, go and light the signals quickly. I doubt whether help can get here in time now, but we might as well be avenged" shouted the Master as Adam came bursting in, half dressed with his hair standing out at all angles.

"The leading cloaked figures have stopped to light torches" Adam said in a hurry. "It can't be for seeing their way now. I think your signalling system has been betrayed. They plan to confuse the other villages long enough to overcome us alone."

"If you can think of a way to bring help quickly I shall be forever in your debt" said the Master climbing into his toughest clothes. "In the meantime, I have a village to defend."

"I think I know a way" said Adam quietly. "What is the signal and where is a torch?" Grabbing a torch out of the hands of a surprised villager, as the Master of Hope explained the signal, Adam ran swiftly between the houses dodging men, women and children streaming in a variety of directions until he came to the foot of the Stairs. Already his old classmates were assembling on the lower steps, keeping close to the wall in view of the one in ten slope towards the edge.

"Out of my way" shrieked Adam as he ploughed through them up the stairs, their cries for information dying away behind him. Now, he thought, would come the test of whether the last year's training had done any good to his fitness. He raced on, keeping one hand out to trace the wall on his left, and the torch well out in front and above him to see the way. About halfway up, he tripped and fell, catching his knee on the tread of the stair. Climbing to his feet, shaking all over he ran on thanking Mother World that it was still dark, making it difficult to see the drop to the fields below. However, the stairs were perfectly dry, and he found after a time that their outwards slope didn't bother him too much.

When he reached the top, puffing and blowing, it took him a few moments to find the striker, and, when he looked up at Hemlock, he nearly forgot the urgency of his purpose. Although he could still see the outline of the bell, he could also see through it. Taking it all in at a glance, he had no time to consider why or what was happening, but he seemed to be looking down a tunnel, at the end of which was a circular disk, containing countless points of rapidly moving white light.

Adam forced his attention back to the immediate problem, and swung the striker against the transparent Bell with all the force he could muster. Twice more he struck it then, waiting a space of five breaths, he struck three more times. He managed to keep the peals ringing out for quite a while and then, worried about the events taking place at the foot of the stairs, he picked up his torch and tottered wearily down the long flight below him. As he went, Adam prayed that his knee wouldn't stiffen before reaching the bottom step at the very least. Already he could see lights all over the World springing up in answer to the Bell's message. A clear call for help had been sent. Whether that help would come in time was quite another matter. As he limped down in the darkness he recalled his last glimpse, just before he had left the platform, of the disk with the little points of light. He realised, just as he had turned away, that within the disk all the points of light were moving rapidly from left to right.

In the meantime, the Patriarch and Inga together were having things very much their own way. It is true that complete surprise had not been achieved, but by sending a dozen confusing light signals all possible help had been delayed. As soon as the main body of the wildmen had assembled on the edge of the village, and Inga had had it explained to her where the food stores were at the centre of the village, the whole force moved forward into the village meeting sporadic and week resistance. Progress slowed as the village absorbed their movements and men wasted time entering individual houses searching for food. To the Patriarch's surprise and increasing worry, the Hope villagers were not defending their territory as they ought to have been doing. Upon reaching the centre of the village and the food stores his worst fears were realised. Around the store was a thin line of defenders, but nothing like the number there should have been if the 'life blood' of the village had been safely inside. The Patriarch felt a little better when the Master of Hope appeared with his retinue of guards.

"Ye're too late Big Fellar" said Inga moving forward to engage the men in front.

In reply the Master swung a hammer with one hand in a blur of speed releasing it straight at Inga. Out of the corner of her eye, Inga saw it coming, but she only just managed to sway out of its path enough to avoid its full force. However, the handle of the hammer caught her ear in passing, whilst the two men immediately behind her were flung to the ground, one rendered unconscious and the other bleeding and moaning.

In the horrified pause that followed the Master picked up a second hammer and said "Don't be so sure, slut!" And turning to the Patriarch he added "Don't you know these animals will turn on you if they succeed in killing us?"

"Take no notice" shouted the Patriarch. "He is only delaying us. Hurry!"

At this point the Bell overhead rang out as Adam strove to warn the other villages.

A growl rose in the throats of the wildmen, which turned into a roar as they surged forward. There was however, limited space between the houses to advance and the leading Wildman, Zibeon, found his club-arm seized in mid swing as if by a vice. He was lifted completely off his feet and the grip transferred to his right leg. Using the yelling man as a flail, the Master of Hope checked the rush before it became unstoppable. It was some time before a way was found to circumvent him. As soon as he saw the defenders at the food store attacked, the Master gave ground and flung the now senseless man to one side. Taking care not to get cut off, the Master's men withdrew to the foot of the stairs. The pursuit slackened slightly as men stayed behind to break into the food store, but a cry went up when it was found to be empty but for a couple of sacks of grain.

Failure to cut off a line of retreat to the stairs was not entirely the fault of the Patriarch, for he had detailed a part of his force to head straight for it, bypassing the village entirely. However, this party had been delayed by coming across food-carrying fugitives from the village. These fugitives, mainly elderly folk and children were powerless to resist and suffered grievously in their twos and threes. However, by the time the attacking party had reached the stairs, all the remaining women and children were safely up and out of the way, in the darkness beyond the torch lights. At the foot of the steps, stood the major proportion of the male adult population of Hope, waiting for the return of their Master. Very soon there came a group of men flying from the village, in the centre of which, could be seen the Master shouting orders, and ducking behind a shield held in front of him, whenever stones were thrown by the wildmen. With the help of the men waiting at the foot of the stairs, the Master broke through the party of attackers, and retired some twenty steps up the flight just out of weapon reach. Star, with four or five guard dogs from Hope on leashes, stood near to the men waiting her chance to use them to good effect.

Urged on by the Patriarch, the wildmen and accompanying Priests searched the village rapidly for food, but at least half of the amount, that had been in Hope at the start of the attack, had been carried out in small quantities by the fleeing population, and by now was dispersed amongst the outlying fields in the dark. The Master had decided, some weeks before, that the central stores of food should be mostly parcelled out to all the villagers, thereby reducing the chances of a possible attack being wholly successful.

The second aim of the attack had been to capture or kill, if necessary, the Master of Hope and thereby rendering the inevitable counter attack far less effective. However, it was sometime before the Patriarch could persuade Inga to abandon the village search, and concentrate on the group up the staircase.

Hemlock had long since stopped ringing and already farmers from outlying areas were arriving on the edge of the village, but hanging back out of the torchlight until their numbers were substantial enough to take on the ransacking wildmen. A huge effort had to be made by the first men to arrive, to prevent the screaming mothers of children, known to have been in the village overnight, from rushing in and being killed in ones and twos. Casualties on both sides were bad but not numerous. Three wildmen lay dead in the village and a further four were seriously wounded. Three elderly Hope villagers had died in the outskirts of Hope trying to escape and another seven wounded. Two defenders had died in defence of their huts and the two women who had refused to leave their husbands, lay dying near the central food store.

Realising that time was running out, and that they could expect no mercy now if they failed, the Patriarch and Inga assembled their men, and, after hurling stones and abuse, charged up the steps. The Master and his men defended as best they could, but they were not anything like as tough as the wildmen who would rush up and grab a villager, deliberately drag him over the edge of the stairs and into the waiting arms of the wildmen below. In this way over a matter of moments they had disposed of six more villagers at the cost of only two of their own. But try as they might the Master himself couldn't be shifted. Adam arrived back just as a lull in the fighting occurred. He was limping now and as tired from emotion as from physical exertion. He shouted encouragement to the Master who was leaning up against the End of the World breathing heavily, blood flowing from several wounds. The Master smiled back whilst Adam shouted down to the wildmen below.

"You are too late!" he shouted. "Help is coming swiftly and what is more your village is on fire!" This last statement was an outright lie but the effect on the wildmen was discernable. Then Adam turned to the Master and those nearest him "Up the stairs" he urged. "Quickly up the stairs everybody. The higher we are the more difficult it will be to get us down. The wildmen won't risk being surrounded …." His voice was drowned by the next attack surging up from below. Adam was struck from behind, and pitched forward in a daze, whilst the sound of barking dogs filled his ears. The villagers were covering their retreat up the stairs by using the guard dogs.

This respite lasted only a few moments, and out of the melee of dogs and men sprang Inga howling with rage; blood from her torn ear splattered all over her shoulder and brawny arm. She seemed to flow up the stairs rather than run and, deflecting a spade blow, she collided with the Master head on. Locked together, the two of them struggled desperately to get a decisive grip. Inga was too bulky for the Master to lift easily, and she wasn't strong enough to risk a straight contest with a club. Back and forth they swayed, while others stood transfixed awaiting the outcome. Inga was desperately trying to keep close to him and trip him up; the Master trying to disentangle himself from her arms so that he could apply his greater strength. No one dared to help, from fear of hitting the wrong antagonist.

Suddenly the Master stopped trying to break away and, gripping Inga round the chest, he summoned all his strength and squeezed. There was a cracking noise, and Inga cried out as her rib cage was subjected to such pressure that the ribs started breaking. The Patriarch, hovering close, waiting his chance to intervene on Inga's behalf, fearing the worst, rushed forward to deal the Master a blow but tripped on his own gown. Then, with fearful strength the Master of Hope lifted Inga off her feet, while she kicked out squealing with fear. Then both Inga and the Master overbalanced and, crashed down at the very edge of the stairs. There followed a noise of further ribs breaking and a curse from the Master, who had crushed his hand against the step. Both the Master and Inga fell heavily to the ground near the bottom step. The curse was cut short as his head struck the step. The onlookers, as if released from a spell, rushed forward to assist the two still figures, pulling them apart with difficulty.

Adam's World stopped reeling about quite so violently and he saw below him a mass of faces. Furthermore, he saw, forming up behind the wildmen and Priests, were about a hundred men and women from other villages, with the Master of Hail co-ordinating them into an organised band. Adam staggered down the stairs and took up a position near the stricken Master of Hope. Sunbright was just beginning, his shadow appearing on the wall behind him.

"Stop everyone and listen to me please" he shouted. But no one took any notice. All eyes were concentrated upon the wildmen and the Priests.

"Kill the scum" shouted one of the newly arrived villagers. A general murmur of approval went through the ranks of men closing in. The wildmen rapidly formed up to face two fronts with the Priests in between.

"No" shrieked Adam. "It's pointless, pointless now. Everything is about to change!"

By now the Master of Hope and Inga had been separated, and carried back to the safety of their supporters" positions. Both were unconscious but, of the two, Inga looked very much the worse. The arrival of the villagers now tipped the balance of strength against the wildmen and priests, although to disarm them was certainly not going to be easy, even now.

The Patriarch made the most of this circumstance. "We will fight to the very last man" he shouted. "Adam, talk to the Master of Hail for all of us."

Adam sat down on the edge of the steps, his legs dangling over the edge and called breathlessly down, "Master, I think there must be a truce. Further fighting can be avoided if everybody stays exactly where they are."

"How can we trust them Adam?" called up the Master of Hail, not really wanting along drawn out battle with additional casualties. The farmers were not used to fighting and the wildmen looked grim and desperate enough to take on several men.

"I think they trust me" called Adam. "Let me talk to them and see what can be agreed."

It took about half an hour to arrange a deal, as all parties sat down to 'lick their wounds' and let tempers cool. In return for bringing the Hope Villagers down off the stairs, the wildmen were to be allowed to occupy the Hall of Voices. But a ring of the strongest villagers would be maintained around them. Those Priests who had also come to Hope, also sat with the wildmen, wondering what was going to become of them.

Whilst these movements were being conducted, Star climbed up the stairs until she was about a quarter of the way to the top, sat down, and began to sing. The sound of her voice floated down, and had a soothing effect on the men, women and children below. Adam stood further down the stairs at the level of the Hope roof tops, and addressed the hundred or so men and women within earshot, and below.

"Everybody, please listen to me" he shouted as loud as he could. "Today is no ordinary day. And I don't mean the battle we have just had. There are about to be many new changes to our World." He paused to cough. Even the low hum of conversation died and everyone listened. "Four weeks from today you will be in a New World, the wonders of which you cannot imagine. Some of these changes have occurred already, but you have been too busy fighting to notice. The lack of food will only be a temporary problem. I will see whether a scheme, to share the surviving stocks, can be arranged."

A boy, whose mother had kept him away from the pageant preparations, arrived panting, having run all the way from School End. He called up to Adam. "Yet another doorway has appeared near the Library of Light, in School House." The boy sat down on the lowest step of the stairs to recover his breath, before continuing. "In addition, the lake is lower than I have ever seen it, and you can see into the lumps. They seem to be full of different kinds of tools. What are they for Adam?"

"I know" said Adam, "or rather I can guess. But I don't know why the lake is lower." Then, holding his head in his hands, he groaned, "Oh 'Hell's Ruin', my head is splitting." Adam glanced up the stairs before adding, "And, if you go and look at Hemlock you will also get a surprise."

"It's too dangerous" said the Patriarch who, in Inga's absence was the spokesman for the wildmen and, of course, his own people the Priests.

"Not for long" said Adam. "Star is singing to the sun and, in a short while, the hill we have had for over a year will go away."

"you're not so high and mighty that you control Mother World yet, Adam" said the Patriarch. "There have been people predicting the End of the World for over a year and nothing more has happened. It's all complete nonsense!"

"I have my information from the Library of Light" said Adam "and by my calculations, the change should happen very soon now."

"I'll believe it when I feel it" snorted the Patriarch. "And, even if it does occur, it doesn't necessarily mean anything."

He didn't have to wait long. Shortly after, the World suddenly lost its hill, the sun suddenly became much brighter and the Bell-ringer, upon reaching Hemlock, found the Bell transparent, just as Adam had said he would. The mood in Hope gradually turned from mourning and gloom, into surprise and amazement. Adam's reputation became impeccable, and Star was asked by a small child if she was 'Evening Star' returned from the Legend. This name caught on, and, after a few days, everyone started calling her that. The wildmen and the Priests were persuaded to send a deputation into Hope suing for peace, and for a long truce lasting out the final days of the Valhalla Haven.

At sundim, a World Council meeting was held in Hope Village. By that time the dead had been carried away by relatives, the wounded patched up, and, if possible, the village restored to order. At the meeting were, the Patriarch (on sufferance); the Master of Happen, Happy and Harp and the Deputy from Hope; a couple of wildmen, Bilhan and Dishon; the Master of Hail; his Deputy; Adam and Star.

The Master of Hail presided over the meeting, the significance of which was not lost on those present, particularly the Patriarch who had been its former chief. The Master of Hail first called for silence, and then asked for a report on the battle from the Hope Deputy, Ebal.

"Well" said Ebal aggressively, "so far we have found twenty bodies. But who knows whether these villains disposed of anyone else on the way here!"

The Master of Hail cut in. "Never mind the disparaging remarks, just state the position at this time."

Ebal glanced at the Patriarch, who disdained to contribute, wishing to remain aloof from the proceedings. "Anyway, twenty two dead for certain" went on Ebal, "and a further ten seriously wounded. On top of that, some sixty five people were wounded less seriously, with such things as broken bones, cuts, gashes and sprains." He looked at one of the wildmen for corroboration. "Do you agree with that total, Bilhan?"

Bilhan scowled. "It's about right" he said sullenly. "Depends how you count Alvan and Inga."

"How is the Master of Hope?" asked Adam, not having the nerve to refer to him as Alvan.

"He's now conscious" said Ebal. "His wife is taking very good care of him." Then he added, "he'll be alright in a day or two."

There were murmurs of pleasure from the other villagers present at this news. Adam turned to Bilhan, "How is Inga?" he asked.

"No good, thanks to Alvan" growled Bilhan. "She's still unconscious and coughing up lots of blood. We think one of the broken ribs has pierced her lungs. In fact" he added glancing up, "Here comes a runner from the house where she is being tended, who may have some news."

Everyone could see from the runner's face that the news was not good. He whispered quickly in the Patriarch's ear. The Patriarch stirred and spoke as though his thoughts were far away.

"Inga is dead" he announced absently. There was a prolonged silence and everyone tried to think of something to say. It was the Master of Hail who eventually broke the silence.

"Inga is hopefully the last casualty of what, in future, will be known as the Battle of the Stairs" he said softly.

The Wildman, Dishon, was about to display his anger when Bilhan restrained him with a gruff word. To the gathering, Bilhan pleaded, "We wish to bury Inga by the lake, as was our custom."

The Master of Hail spoke quietly, "It shall be arranged as you wish, Bilhan. We are all sorry that you have lost an able leader."

"I can imagine" said Bilhan icily, making the most of the sympathy present. But before he could develop this theme, the Master of Hail interrupted him sharply.

"Could I just remind you, that she was leading a violent attack, on a village full of children, that she thought was undefended." There was a prolonged silence as this sunk home. Then he continued. "Now will everybody please listen to what Adam, here, has to say. It's most important and, when you have listened and asked any necessary questions, you must all go and tell the villagers in your respective communities, and any farmers you meet, what you have heard."

"Thank you" began Adam. "I started to explain this morning about the World changes that are about to talk place. In the …."

The Patriarch interrupted, "Have we got to listen to all this rubbish again" he said testily. The Master of Hail's voice now turned menacing. "If anyone else interrupts Adam, and I mean anyone, for whatever reason other than to ask for clarification, I shall have him removed from this meeting." He motioned Adam to proceed.

"In the remaining days there is much to do" Adam continued. "All ill feeling and revenge must be put aside, forever if possible, but at least until the present important matters are dealt with."

He looked particularly at the Masters of Hail and Happy, who had clearly been at 'daggers drawn' since the morning's fighting.

"At the end of the next four weeks we shall have to move out of our homes. I don't know to where, or quite how, but I'm sure that that will be made known to us. Therefore all farming can cease now, and every family must individually prepare for the trip." Adam turned to the Patriarch "Do you know why Hemlock has changed? What does the voice lock there conceal?"

"It is a door to the outside of the World" said the Patriarch suddenly horrified by his own blasphemy. "More that that I cannot say" he added quickly. There was a gasp from his audience at hearing this disclosure from the lips of the Patriarch himself. Adam noticed that the Patriarch hadn't said 'more than that I do not know' and he wondered at the time whether the crafty old Priest wasn't, even now, withholding something from the Council. However, he let the matter drop.

"My guess is that the tools in the lumps are for the New World" continued Adam, "but the additional doorway near the Library of Light requires investigation, and I would propose myself for the task. Would any of the Council wish to accompany me? I shall need the Council's authority to remove the guards at the Library."

It was an indication of the shifting of power that no one questioned Adam's initiative, and only the Master of Happen thought it wise to send his Deputy and the Priest Heman with him, to dismiss the guard and explore.

"Has the hill gone for good?" asked the Master of Happen whose village suffered most from the changes of gradient.

"No" replied Adam. "The hill will be absent for one week. Then it will return for three weeks at the end of which we shall be at our new World. Presumably we shall leave through Hemlock and I suspect Molock as well."

Adam's thoughts shifted from what was about to happen to what, recently, was to have happened. "Oh dear" he said apologetically, "I fear we have not had the Pageant Day we were expecting. I had planned to announce a Change, not a fight a battle. Never mind, the Pageant will have to wait."

Adam looked at the Master of Hail "I would suggest, sir, that an evacuation plan is prepared by each village. The Villages of Happy and Harp can be used by people in transit. This is absolutely essential" he continued forestalling a question he could see coming. "The Pilot …. er …Mother World is not going to let us stay here. I know that for certain."

"What is happening in the Ghost Worlds?" asked the Deputy of Hail.

"I don't know" said Adam. "But I want to go to the Library of Light to try and find out. Perhaps they too have had fighting." Adam sighed and looked out over the fields in which could be seen the odd piece of flag and other indications of the now almost forgotten Pageant. It was odd, he thought, how everything could look pretty well the same as it had always done, and yet feel so entirely different.

Chapter Fourteen – Preparing for the End

During the weeks of training with his school friends, and organising groups of adults and with no pilot to talk to, Adam had almost forgotten his excitement at manipulating the controls of the Library of Light, and receiving answers to his questions. Now, as he sat down in one of the chairs in front of a screen, the feeling returned to him.

The Happen Deputy Master, Zoavan and Priest Heman, stood beside him, at a loss to know what was going on, and not a little impressed by the assured way in which Adam approached the controls. Calling up the Valhalla Inn, which he found now to be possible, Adam could see no one in the Library, so he tried the next world, the Valhalla Jonah. Here, Adam was lucky, for there was a woman, Naomi, in one of the chairs talking to someone from the Valhalla Night. His appearance was a pleasant surprise to Naomi, since no communication had been possible with the Valhalla Haven or any other ghost world for nearly a year and a half. The grass covered worlds had been far less affected by the changes, that they too had undergone, and life continued there very much as before. According to Naomi on the Valhalla Jonah, the Valhalla King had been in communication for a while but recently had lost contact. Valhalla Over and Valhalla Pass were now in touch again, but food riots had occurred. But the other Worlds were not Adam's principal concern so, as soon as he could distract Zoavan from exchanging news with them, he called up the Pilot with the interrogation routine. He addressed it directly, as he had done before.

"Pilot, I want some more information."

"State your questions clearly" answered the Pilot instantly.

The other two men looked around, mystified, for the origin of the voice. It seemed to come from no single source.

"The slope of the World has gone again. What is happening and why?"

"Again, I assume you are referring to the cessation of de-acceleration" replied the Pilot. "The units in the group of which you are part are now breaking up to take up their proper stations in the chosen solar system."

"Will you explain, in very simple language, what units are, why they are breaking up and what 'proper stations' means?"

"Look at the screen in front of you" said the Pilot.

On the screen appeared a central point of light with twelve smaller points of light circling the central point.

"This" said the Pilot, "is a description of the solar system you are about to enter. There are twelve major planets circling the central sun."

Ten new points of light, in a line and close together, emerged from the edge of the screen and converged on the circling points.

"These are the ten space vehicles which comprise some of the Valhalla series. Already, half of the Valhalla Over and Pass have detached themselves and moved to orbit the outer planet of the system, from which they will send all messages and information back to the origin of the enterprise. In two days time, half of each of the Valhalla Jonah, King, Light, Moss and Night will move close to the central sun. Their task is to set up the required 'field' in this sector of space for the expedition which is to follow. The remaining halves of these vessels and the whole of the Valhalla Haven, Inn, and Queen will then proceed to the planet which has been selected for colonisation."

"Is the Valhalla Haven really moving?" asked Adam who was still having difficulty with this concept and wanted direct confirmation of it.

"Yes, relative to the solar system nearby."

"Why can't we feel it moving?" Heman spoke for the first time.

"You will only perceive changes in movement" said the Pilot.

"It's very awkward" said Adam. "There is obviously so much going on that we don't know about, that we cannot phrase our questions accurately enough." Adam thought for a moment. "How long has the Valhalla Haven been moving" he asked.

"Nearly 7870 crop growing cycles or years."

Heman laughed. "Either we have been moving since before The Beginning, or The Lost Ages were a great deal longer than the records suggest. My goodness, I wonder what else we've got wrong."

Adam nodded his agreement and continued his questions.

"Where is the Valhalla Inn?" he asked.

"Four hundred miles away."

None of the three men present knew what a mile was, so Adam asked a further question.

"What is this distance compared to the length of the Valhalla Haven?"

"If by length you mean distance from engine to telescope then the answer is about 160 times as far."

While Adam, Father Heman and Zoavan were absorbing this, the screen in front of them went blank, only to come alive again almost immediately with nine dots of light placed in a graceful arc. Both Adam and Heman cried out together "The marks on Hemlock!"

"Except that the tenth point is on the Bell to represent the vessel we are in" said Adam. "Perhaps we had better find out more about some of the details in the World now." He addressed the Pilot again. "At the top of the Stairs at Bell End are two Bells, 'M' lock and 'O' lock" said Adam trying to be as precise as possible. "What are they for other than ringing out the quarter days, and to where do the voice locks lead?"

"Your questions are unclear. The mechanism at the top of the Stairs, 'M' lock and 'O' lock, are multiple doors to enable properly clothed engineers to leave or enter the vessel during the journey. They are necessary because there is no air outside the Valhalla Haven." Then the Pilot added, "The airlocks only 'ring' when they are sealed."

But Adam had now lost interest in the airlocks as bells. "How will we leave Valhalla Haven if there is no air?" asked Adam anxiously.

"You will not leave through the 'airlocks' replied the Pilot.

Adam and Zoavan looked at each other in surprise. "Then how will we leave?" asked Adam

"Through the two circular doors in the wall that contains the 'sun'."

"I think it means School House and Clearance" said Adam after a moments thought. "I don't understand that at all. Never mind, lets move on. What is Clearance … no, what is the place where we all have to spend a night around our fifteenth birthdays?"

"Genetic and health checking station and short term population control" replied the Pilot blandly.

"That doesn't mean much to me either" said Adam. But a further question on the same aspect of World geography was necessary to ease his conscience.

"Will this procedure be necessary at our destination 'planet'?"

"No" replied the Pilot, much to Adam's relief. "It was only necessary during the journey to prevent genetic deterioration of human stock."

But Adam had stopped listening. He was frantically thinking of other more important things to ask. "To where does the recently opened door lead?"

"It leads to the Services Corridor."

"Why has it opened now?"

"Because you will need to enter this area for the landing."

"What happens if we refuse to leave our homes?" asked Zoavan, before Adam could tell him he had asked this question once before, although in a slightly different form.

"There will be no air left in the Valhalla Haven" said the Pilot bluntly.

Adam turned to Zoavan and the Priest "I think we ought to go and look in the new passage" he said. But then a thought struck him, which he had meant to put in the form of a question, some moments before. He remembered the lack of any contact with the Valhalla Queen.

"Why do we not get any answer from the Valhalla Queen?" he asked.

"The inhabitants of the Valhalla Queen cannot talk" was the reply. "They live in water all the time."

After the flying creatures reported on Valhalla's Over and Pass nothing would have surprised Adam.

"So that would explain it" said Zoavan. "All the Worlds are in good order." He hadn't meant this statement to be a question but the Pilot took it as such.

"No. The Valhalla Jonah has defective circuiting in the engine control system. The back up circuits have also failed."

None of them knew what to make of this.

"Will they be alright?" Zoavan enquired.

"If by that you mean the humans within the Valhalla Jonah, then the answer depends upon whether the vessel can be manoeuvred for landing. This will only be known in fourteen days time."

Suddenly Adam was reminded of the rhyme "Clap a hand over hand poor old Joe". He had always thought that this referred to Engineer Joe, but now a better interpretation presented itself. It did refer to Engineer Joe, but it had once been Engineer Jonah, and the whole story referred to some repair incident that had occurred sometime after the Beginning. Apparently, those repairs had not been entirely successful.

To give themselves a break, Adam, Father Heman and Zoavan set off to explore the new door and corridor, at the bottom of the little staircase to the Library of Light. If one walked from the Library of Books up the passage and turned left you entered the new passage (turning right at the same point brought you to the foot of the staircase to the Library of Light). The three men walked slowly down this new passage until they came to a circular door rather like that on the outer entrance to School House. It was partly open and swung when pushed to reveal a long Corridor stretching out into the distance. The further end of the Corridor, which was square in cross section, could not be seen because of the natural curvature of the World whose surface the floor followed. The walls of the corridor were very different from each other. The wall on the left had side – that is – the wall through which lay the World, was lined with giant blank screens, such as the ones in the Library of Light, each about two strides square, interspaced with doors every thirty strides. Each door had lettering over it and was closed with no handle or obvious method of opening it. The right hand wall was lined with what looked like low beds set vertically in the wall about one stride apart. Adam was wondering how anybody could lie down in such a bed when he remembered that when the hill existed in Valhalla Haven, it was possible to lie or lean quite comfortably against a previously vertical wall.

They walked slowly down the corridor reading the names above the doors and seeking further features. The first six doors all had the word 'Atmosphere' over them and underneath a series of different words – Temperature, Humidity, Chemical Composition, Biological Composition, Pressure and Ancillaries.

The next seven doors had the words Power Source over them and underneath Drive Control, Fuel, Position Control and then a separate sub section for Internal Heat Source – Temperature, Radiation, Clock Sequence, and Maintenance Cycles.

Then there followed similar groups of doors covering Soil Condition, Water quality, Telescope, Control Rooms A & B, Airlocks and so on. Adam had counted nearly a hundred doors before the two of them reached the furthest end of the corridor. At this end, too, there was a circular door which they had difficulty in opening, even though instructions for it were printed on the wall close by. Passing through the door, they found themselves in Clearance and had, by now, walked halfway round the circumference of the world. Walking back down the Corridor, they noticed twenty further doors set in the ceiling, and clearly only available for use when the wall, containing the beds, was a floor.

As they neared the end of the Corridor from which they first set out, the world gave a lurch beneath their feet. Rushing back to the Library who should they find there, but Eliphaz, using the interrogation routine. He cut off his questioning and left quickly, when Adam asked him what he was seeking.

Adam asked the Pilot what was happening.

"Minor course correction" it said. "There is, however, a complete failure in the ancillary control circuiting of the Valhalla Jonah. Her course is now diverging from the main group. There is no need for undue alarm. I am now taking over external control and will manoeuvre her using the Main Drive circuits only. In the meantime, I would advise no contact with the occupants of the Valhalla Jonah, who may be emotionally disturbed by the current turn of events."

The Pilot continued to give reassurance, in what Adam recognised as language standard for a variety of emergency situations. The Master Builder seemed to have thought of most things, and emergencies of different kinds would have been planned for.

"This is terrible" said Zoavan. "Everything permanent and stable that I ever knew, suddenly becomes temporary and not what it seems." He turned to go, "I don't think I want to know anymore, Adam. You stay if you like but I'll go and tell the Council about the Corridor."

"I'll come with you" said Heman, "I must report to the Patriarch."

They left quickly leaving Adam putting further questions to the Pilot.

As it happened, Zoavan and Father Heman didn't miss much in the way of question and answer because, shortly afterwards, the Pilot stopped answering Adam's enquiries on 'Interrogation', and for a quarter of an hour remained silent. Adam use the dictionary to look up a few words, tried to use the telescope without success, and was just about to leave, when the voice, he now knew so well, spoke again.

"I must interrupt your use of this Library, to give you instructions regarding the landing procedures. Are you prepared to notify everyone in your vessel?"

"Yes" said Adam. "What are the instructions?"

"First of all you should know the general position" said the Computer. "I have linked all the Valhalla Series Vessels together electronically, with the exception of Valhalla Jonah who has defective circuits. This vessel, the Valhalla Haven, being the last of the group, will make each course correction, each change of altitude and each internal adjustment fractionally after the other vessels whose Master Computers are now subordinate to this vessel. As of this moment, instructions are being given to humans in each Library and, for those vessels whose Library is currently empty, a siren is being sounded to summon humans to their Library. It is not, therefore, necessary for you to make other vessels aware of landing instructions, and I am disconnecting the communications network between them forthwith."

Adam sat back in the chair and prepared to absorb the instructions.

Over the following week, Adam had little time to reflect or be worried about the future. However, Adam, like most people in the Valhalla Haven had imagined, insofar as anyone had thought, that the End of the World was to be some kind of mystical experience, with Paradise opening up before him. For people to be told they would have to leave their homes, and move out into the unknown, came as a hard shock to many of them. Village Masters found themselves inundated with unanswerable questions such as 'why should we move at all', 'what can we take' or 'how much can we take'. More enquiries, Adam reflected, arose over the farm livestock than arose over physical inanimate objects. These usually took the form of wanting to know more about the destination conditions, and whether food had to be taken. These questions, for which the Masters couldn't even guess an answer, were referred back to him. Evening Star, for even Adam found himself calling her this, first as a joke, but eventually for real, acted as a link between the Masters, the wildmen and the Priests. It was an exacting task, and couldn't have been carried out for very long. But then it wasn't required for very long, and by the end of the week following the recent change, most people had made what preparations they were going to make and when the hill returned on schedule, they settled down to wait out the passing of the next three weeks. At about this time, Adam began to notice other subtle changes in the World. The days became slightly longer, as measured by the sand clocks, and he felt a little heavier. What these alterations were for, not even Adam knew for certain, but he guessed they were to prepare everyone for the conditions to be found on the planet to which they were going.

In Adam's view, all would have been well, had it not been for the Priesthood, who were allowed to disperse when the wildmen had been escorted back to Hell Village. The Priesthood were now very much out of favour, and the Patriarch had lost first his authority, and now face, in front of the people when he had challenged Adam's control of the World changes. Not even the wildmen would listen to him anymore, and he was blamed for much of the misfortune that had befallen them, with some justification, many people said. In the meantime, the Master of Hail made it clear to the wildmen that their fate hung upon the good behaviour of the group over the coming weeks. And so, with very little to lose and much to gain, the Patriarch set his face against the best endeavours of Adam and the Village Masters, and many of the Priesthood supported him. It was in Happen Village that Eliphaz, now no longer addressed as the Patriarch, first caused a minor disturbance by preaching in the Village square. His message had an invidious appeal to those who would listen to him.

"Villagers of Happen" called out Eliphaz, "you are being tricked. Believe me, I know."

A few of the villagers sauntered over to listen to him.

"You may have disagreed with my connection with the wildmen but cannot deny my greater knowledge of the past!"

"What has the past got to do with being tricked?" sneered one of the villagers. "And who's talking about tricks anyway?"

"Did you know" shouted Eliphaz "that there has been a hill before in Mother World?"

This was indeed news to the villagers and more people joined the throng around the Priest.

"You don't suppose" said Eliphaz in his most persuasive voice "That there haven't been many changes like this before, do you? And, what is more there will be again. But that's not to say that they herald the End of the World."

"So what's the trick?" persisted the villager in a slightly less aggressive manner.

"Well you are all being asked to move out of your houses soon, aren't you?"

"Well?"

"When you have moved out what do you think is going to happen to your houses, your crops and your livestock?"

There was a general murmuring amongst the crowd. Several arguments began between villagers. One of the latest arrivals on the scene answered the question put by Eliphaz.

"We won't need our houses and farms any more." The villager didn't sound very convinced by his own statement.

"You won't be allowed them any more" thundered Eliphaz. "You poor fools. If Mother World wanted anyone to move, do you really think she would use a fifteen year old boy as a mouthpiece! Where's the sense you were born with, noble villagers of Happen. Once you move out, others will move in. Then what will you do? You are being tricked by those who are taking advantage of your ignorance and fear of the changes."

Such talk was dangerously attractive to a significant proportion of the populace, since it conformed to the beliefs on which they had been raised. It was a credible story for those who had no learning, and whose only contact with the various manifestations of change, was the slope, or hill, which kept appearing. It was also the lazy man's justification, for it meant merely staying put, and continuing as before. As a result of these and other reasons, Eliphaz and his fellow Priests raised quite a following in a very short time.

A week after the onset of de-acceleration, Adam and his girl, Evening Star, were lying in the grass near Adam's home, taking a well earned rest. Companion lay near them pretending to be asleep. Neither Adam nor Evening Star had had very much time to themselves for a number of weeks. Although very much in love, they had agreed to delay getting married, until the Valhalla Haven had arrived at this 'planet' place predicted by the Pilot and the future was more certain.

"I think I would have to spend a year in that Library before I even began to understand what is going on" Adam was saying. "But I think I see what the 'men marching' are now."

"The Valhalla Haven is one of hundreds of these Worlds all travelling somewhere and ten of them have broken off from the rest to stop at this 'planet' place" said Evening Star.

"That would explain the 'count upon your fingers as they come and go' " said Adam. "I suspect the whole column was put together in tens as well."

"What do you suppose the 'one or two above and below' are?"

"Perhaps they tell the seven hundred which way to go, and keep them in line, just as Father Zepho used to keep the children in line when we went for walks from the School."

"And the Valhalla Jonah has been like a naughty school boy and won't behave itself" laughed Evening Star.

"Well at least the Valhalla Queen is alright" said Adam. "It didn't occur to me that life could be so different. I suppose I should have done after the odd creatures in some of the other Worlds."

Evening Star rolled over on to her back and picked out another blade of grass to chew. "Why are we going to the 'planet' place Adam? I still don't see why we can't stay here for ever. I'm a bit frightened at the thought of Paradise and I find this waiting unbearable."

"Try not to worry, I asked the Pilot why we were travelling. I didn't really understand the answer except that our journey is not the major purpose of the … the … Caravan" said Adam.

"I guess I don't mind as long as it is somewhere not too unpleasant and we're together." Evening Star looked at Adam meaningfully.

But Adam's thoughts were far away. "I asked what a planet was, and the Pilot told me about things called rivers which are made of flowing water and land sticking right up into the air with white tops, and groups of trees so large it takes several days to walk across from one side to the other. And he also mentioned something called the sky, which I don't understand at all." Adam's eyes were shining as he tried to imagine it. He turned to look at Evening Star. She was lying stretched out beside him with her eyes shut. The sight of her lying there with a provocative smile on her face made him forget his original train of thought completely. After several moments he said, with a twinkle in his eyes, "I haven't really had time to tell you how beautiful you are."

"Nor the inclination" replied Evening Star feigning a huff.

"Oh, I've wanted to, many times but there have always been so many people about. It's very difficult not to notice your lovely figure."

"What about my superb mental faculties?" said Evening Star accusingly. "You men are all the same."

"I've got similar mental faculties too you know" said Adam pretending to be indignant. "But very dissimilar physical features I'm glad to say. Would you like me to kiss you now or when I've told you how marvellous your singing was after the battle."

Evening Star threw a tuft of grass at him, and kissed him before and after.

"What are we going to do about Eliphaz?" she enquired. "He's going to cause no end of trouble when we try and get everybody into the Service Corridor."

"Don't worry" said Adam. "I have a feeling people won't have much choice. I don't know how the Pilot intends to do it, but I have very detailed instructions for those that do arrive in the Service Corridor, and what we are to do upon 'landing', whatever that may be. Apparently, we have to stay in the Service Corridor for a week, whilst we are given some kind of protection against the new air we shall be breathing."

"I still think Eliphaz is going to give us trouble" said Evening Star.

"You worry too much. Give us another kiss."

Later, Evening Star said "Adam for goodness sake I can't breathe."

"What do you think your nose is for" said Adam and kissed her again.

Quite a lot later, they got up and walked slowly back to Adam's home.

Chapter Fifteen – The Downfall of Eliphaz

Just before sunbright, two weeks later, Adam was standing in the doorway of his home looking out over the fields, with a scarcely contained excitement. Behind him, Kenan and Jabal his brothers, and Miriam his Mother were finishing a meagre breakfast. Most of the family's valuable possessions lay packed up, in piles, around them. "Well" he thought "today's the day! Everything still looks more or less the same. I wonder what will happen first? I hope I have got the days right, because I'm going to look very foolish if I haven't."

For the hundredth time, Adam went over in his mind the events of the last few days, to reassure himself that events were reaching a climax. Emotional tensions in the World population would, by now, have reached explosive point had it not been that two days ago, villagers began to complain of feeling listless and tired without reason. For a while, it was put down to the general lack of anything constructive to do, but it soon became so marked, that it was recognised as a deliberate effect imposed upon them, presumably to prevent them over-reacting to forthcoming events. It was Eliphaz who first connected the lethargy with the water supply and, from then on, refused both food and drink from anyone. His followers remained substantial in number, and only in Hope Village, where memories were still sharp, was he now most unwelcome.

Adam knew that the Master of Hope, now fully recovered from the concussion but still with a heavily bandaged hand, was continuing to vigorously oppose Eliphaz's influence in every possible way. He was touring the other villages and outlying farms countering all the arguments put forward by the Chief Priest.

The air had recently become noticeably thinner and cooler; the slope of the World had become, if anything, steeper; and the sun dimmer. At the same time, artificial lighting came on in School House, and the lighting in the Library, Clearance and the long Service Corridor became brighter, and the air warmer. A slight breeze out of the School House and Clearance door, indicated that the air within was being maintained at a higher pressure. It now became increasingly difficult for Eliphaz to maintain that nothing was going to happen. At last, his followers slowly began to fall away. Whether this was due to the signs; persuasion by the Masters, or the general apathy created by the contaminated water supply, was not known, but people seriously contemplated the move to School End. This was good news.

Then, at about midnight, this last night, during which he hadn't slept at all, Adam and his family had detected several violent movements of the World beneath their feet. Between each movement the slope of the ground died away for a few moments only to rear up again and remain as before. Gradually, the movements became less and less severe, until they were barely detectable to the balancing mechanism in the human ear. Finally, the ground became level and remained that way.

Adam stood at the doorway to his house watching and listening. "So what was to happen next?" thought Adam, "I feel a bit tired, but am I ready for whatever I'm called upon to do? Is my family ready?" Adam turned to find his brothers right behind him.

"When do we leave?" asked Jabal, in a voice that said he believed it had to be done, and rather wanted to get it over with.

"I don't know" confessed Adam. "My instructions from the Pilot had three parts. There were instructions for marshalling people and installing them in the Service Corridor, instructions for their behaviour during their stay there, and instructions as to how they could be got out of the Corridor, onto the surface of the planet, and fed for a sufficient length of time for them to find their own feet." He paused and then continued less confidently. "There was little, however, that the pilot gave me of by way of advice, as to how to persuade some five hundred people to abandon their homes, and many of their belongings. In spite of my assurances to Evening Star, I am far from happy about the effect of Eliphaz's recent preaching. I'm just hoping that the Master Builder had a plan to deal with this problem."

"He seems to have been fairly thorough in other respects" put in Kenan. "However, I shall be interested to see how he tackles this."

"Mark you" he added "with this latest listlessness from the water supply, most people seem to have lost their ability to object to anything."

"Will you three stop chattering and come and help me tidy up a bit" called their Mother from the kitchen area.

"Mother!" sighed Kenan, "We will not be coming back, you know. We don't need to clear anything up."

"My house will be left tidy" insisted his Mother firmly. The rest of her remarks were interrupted by a very loud voice from outside. So loud, indeed, that it could not possibly have been produced by a human. The family immediately scrambled outside to listen and to find out from where it came.

Even outside, the origin of the voice was obscure but it was pitched high and clear, booming out across the World with a message for everyone. Adam stood absolutely still, shushed his Mother who was asking for explanations, and concentrated on the contents of the message.

" ……this message. It affects every living creature in the World" the voice was saying over and over again. "Listen to this message. It affects every living creature in the World." While Adam waited for the message itself to begin he noticed other families living nearby also standing outside, and still, taking in the announcement. The voice paused, and then proceeded to instruct them.

"Everyone is to go to either Clearance or the Library where they will be assigned places in the long passage called the Services Corridor. You should take with you every living animal you can, and all the personal possessions of other kinds, for which there is a space. You will not be returning to your homes. Any who insist on remaining in their homes will shortly die because the air is being removed from the World and will not return. You need have no fear. Everything has been provided for. Everyone is safe. Whatever you feel or hear in the coming hours need not alarm you unduly. Have patience and fortitude so that you, your children, your livestock and other possessions may arrive shortly in a new and even more wonderful World."

There was a pause and then the voice started all over again.

"Well" said Adam, "there's part of your answer, Jabal. We start moving now."

He moved back inside the house so that he didn't have to shout to make himself heard. His brothers followed.

"I'm going to be needed at School House. For some reason, the voice hasn't advised people to take a seven day supply of food with them. I must make sure that as many as can, do" said Adam. "I shall go ahead if you two will see that Mother and all our possessions arrive there within the hour." Adam paused at the doorway before departing. "Thank goodness the waiting is over" he said smiling for the first time in several weeks. "Now I can get my teeth into something."

As Adam set out to School House in the gloom of a dim sun and chilly air, he could see other families setting out from their homes, in many cases driving their livestock before them.

It had been left to the Village Masters to see that everyone left their homes, and that no looting took place. Only a few of the elderly and sick had to be forced to leave home or carried on litters. Within half an hour of the message, families were beginning to arrive at School End in large numbers.

Evening Star stood in Clearance, and Adam in the Library, guiding people through and explaining that the vertical beds would soon be necessary as well as useful, and that each person should have one to himself. The animals would have to take their chance without bedding, but they too were very docile in spite of the way they were chivvied and pushed about.

Adam was just beginning to think that the worst was over, when the Master of Hail came in looking for him.

"Adam, there has been an incident at Happy a short while ago. Eliphaz seems to have gone mad and is determined to make things difficult for us if he can. He has struck Cheran a terrible blow with his staff, and began cursing your name and swearing revenge. He left with his fellow Priest, Nahath, shouting "Tell that little upstart and braggart that I have gone where I can wreck his schemes. Cheran is being carried in now, but he is in a very bad way. Where Eliphaz and Father Nahath are, I don't know."

"So they have finally fallen out" reflected Adam, recalling that it was Cheran, the Master of Happy village, who had betrayed the other village Masters plans.

Adam leant against the vertical bars in the School House wall, and racked his brains as to what Eliphaz had meant. "He couldn't have been referring to Hell, because most of the wildmen had arrived at School House. The Hall of Voices had been silent, ever since the Library of Light had opened. I am already at School House, so Eliphaz couldn't be planning to wreck the Library; Hope is deserted; Evening Star is surrounded by too many people to be in danger; her parents and my mother are already here; Companion is with me … hm … oh No! Molock and Hemlock!

"Good grief" gasped Adam. "He's gone to open the voice locks on the bells. Which one I wonder? Hemlock would be the nearest. If he opens that lock before everyone is inside the Corridor, we've all had it." He looked round for someone to take his place, saw Zepho and after giving him quick instructions, called to Companion and ran off towards Bell End.

As it happened, Eliphaz and Nahath hadn't gone directly to Bell End. They had first gone round to 'Clearance' hoping to get into the Corridor without too much trouble. Evening Star saw them storming along the edge of the lake, avoiding the stretches of mud and slime. "Here comes trouble" she thought but, not knowing what had transpired in Happy Village, she assumed that they had come to grudgingly take up their places in the long corridor.

Brusquely pushing some farmers aside, Eliphaz climbed through the outer door of Clearance. "Out of my way, Girl" he shouted, while Nahath climbed through the door behind him. Evening Star began, "Welcome, Patriarch and Father Nahath, you have been allocated ….." But Eliphaz interrupted her, "Allocation? – nonsense – I am here to give a last warning to these farmers who are being tricked by that jumped up boyfriend of yours." And before Evening Star could do anything to prevent it, Eliphaz and Nahath had disappeared down the corridor talking to anyone who would listen.

Evening Star dare not leave the door, and her task of guiding people in. She could hear much shouting and the sound of angry voices moving slowly, down the corridor, and further away from 'Clearance'. As she was trying to decide what she should do, a girl known to her arrived with her family. With the father's agreement, Evening Star sent the girl round by the lake, all the way to School House, to warn Adam of what was happening.

As it turned out, this intelligent action proved quite unnecessary because, a few moments after the departure of the girl, she could see a crowd of angry villagers and farmers coming down the Corridor towards her. In the centre of the crowd were Eliphaz and Nahath, practically apoplectic with rage, being dragged along without any courtesy or regard for their status. Evening Star stood aside while the two priests were literally thrown out, and back into the World, and told not to return until they could be more co-operative. A few villagers remained at the door to see that this instruction was followed. Evening Star expected the two priests to hang around outside Clearance and to reconsider their position but, on the contrary, they strode off glaring and muttering to themselves.

As a result of this failed attempt at disrupting the move of the population into the corridor, the Priests were delayed somewhat, and eventually decided to make for Molock rather than Hemlock.

In the meantime, Adam was glad that the 'hill' had gone. He ran straight across the fields and ridges, with Companion, alongside, easily keeping up with him. It was an eerie journey for most of the way, with deserted paths and houses standing silent in the gloom. Overhead, he could just see the other side of the World, but no friendly lights flickered there. An abandoned cat sat on one of the ridges, and watched them inscrutably as they passed. As he neared Hope Village, Adam stopped and stared up at Hemlock. He could see nothing moving on either stair or platform. His eyes moved upwards, to the Bell 'Molock', far above and the seemingly tiny stairs to it. About half way up, were two little dots moving slowly towards the top. With a curse Adam set off again, and joining the path to Hail Village just outside Hope, ran with all possible speed round the great curve of the World. He realised, as he ran, that the air was becoming far chillier than usual. The cold was something no inhabitant of the Valhalla Haven was accustomed to.

Reaching the foot of the stairs to Molock, Adam paused for breath. Companion sniffed around his feet, impatient to be off again. Adam waited only a few moments, considering whether to take the dog with him. Having decided that his need for the dog, was greater than the risk for the dog, he started up the stairs with Companion trotting up behind him. Having just run across a good half of the world with only limited rests, he soon had to slow to a walk, his chest heaving in the thin air. On and on he drove himself, hoping desperately that something would delay Eliphaz and Nahath, and that they would have difficulty opening the lock. That Eliphaz knew how to open it, Adam was certain, although how he knew was unclear. Shortly before Adam and his dog reached the top, Molock rang out through the gloom, not sharp and clear, but with a dull and flat tone.

Looking up, Adam saw Eliphaz standing waiting for him. Nahath stood at his side, hands on hips, still as a statue.

Eliphaz shouted to Adam, "So you have come alone have you, upstart? What a pity, I had hoped there would be a few more to witness my last triumph." Eliphaz was desperately trying to control a towering rage. His eyes were wild and clothes dishevelled. He was positively trembling with emotion.

Adam sank down on the steps just below the platform, struggling to regain his breath, while Companion looked at him questioningly for instructions. "Well at least" thought Adam, "he hasn't opened the lock yet. Perhaps I can delay him by talking. If he starts to open the lock, then somehow my friend" and he glanced at Companion beside him, "somehow, my good and faithful friend, you and I will have to push him over the edge even if it means going over with him!"

Adam stirred to stand up but Eliphaz shouted.

"Don't move, boy! I can open the lock in a trice now for I have released all the mechanisms, with the single exception of some words of command."

All kinds of thoughts flashed through Adam's head. "Surely the Master Builder wouldn't have made it too easy to open the locks and endanger the World … But maybe towards the end He would …. There must be at least two doors … But maybe Eliphaz knows how to open both of them."

Adam desperately hoped that, back in the Service Corridor, Zepho would obey his last instruction that, should the air pressure begin to decrease rapidly, before

Adam's return, he should shut the door of School House and Clearance. It had only recently dawned on Adam why these doors were circular and sealable.

Eliphaz ranted on. "Well, Adam, it is perhaps justice that you should be here alone. We shall die together, you and I; whilst the rest of the World will know, when they die an instant or two later, that you had failed and I have triumphed." He paused for breath, and then continued. "When I open the lock, either all the air of the World will rush out, or those demons they speak about will rush in. Which will it be, Adam the Wise? You and I know only too well, don't we? We both spoke with the voice in the Library of Light, didn't we?"

Adam glanced back down the stairs. There was still no sign of the men Adam had asked Zepho to send after him.

"I think you are a fool Eliphaz" said Adam, still playing for time. "You try to challenge forces and plans about which you, and indeed all of us, know little. Nothing you can do will prevent the Valhalla Haven from landing successfully. Do you really think the Master Builder would have any part of his schemes capable of being put at risk by a renegade priest? I think not. And beware Eliphaz, the Builder of the World may be dead but his mechanisms live on. With their help the Builder can reach out over thousands of years and strike you down."

Eliphaz threw back his head and laughed, a cold, hard, bitter laugh. "Well let's see what he can do about this" he shouted. Before Adam or Companion could move, Eliphaz turned to face Molock and said in a loud voice. "I wish to enter the first chamber." There was a click and a hiss, and Adam was on his feet just in time to see the whole Bell, which was hinged, swing rapidly outwards away from the wall knocking Eliphaz backwards over the edge of the platform, as the air in the lock forced its way out to mingle with the air at a much lower air pressure in the Valhalla Haven. With a choking cry, Eliphaz disappeared over the edge. Nahath, who was standing further back waiting to hold the lock door open, grabbed it as it swung towards him, and stood looking stupidly at the vanishing figure of his chief. As Adam leapt onto the platform, Nahath looked as if he might jump rather than face Adam and his dog alone. Adam took the lock door from him, slammed it shut and said quietly.

"Don't follow him Father Nahath. Eliphaz was prepared to throw your life away and everyone elses out of fear and revenge. Look around you, this old world is dying but you don't have to die with it, come and see the wonderful New World we have been promised."

Slowly, surprise and horror left Nahath's eyes. He was having difficulty in believing what he had just witnessed. Finally, he shrugged his shoulders and reluctantly allowed Adam to lead him down the long flight of steps in preparation for a trip back across a darkening, silent World.

Chapter Sixteen – The Landing

At the foot of the stairs to Molock, they were met by the party of men sent out, by Zepho, to look for and help Adam. At Nahath's insistence, they took Eliphaz, whose broken body they found on the path outside the Hall of Silence, and quickly buried him in the fields nearby. Then the whole party set off back to the School End of the World.

On the way, the party gathered up a stray chicken and a young puppy, and took them along to School House. There was no sign of the cat that Adam had seen earlier.

They had all reached Halfway Path when the silence was broken by a shrill whine, emanating from somewhere high up Bell End. It rapidly built up in power, until it was most unpleasant to hear. Adam wondered, as they all staggered along blocking their ears as best they could, how many other automatic mechanisms there were for ensuring that a reluctant population moved into the Service Corridor at the appointed time.

When the party reached Clearance, Evening Star showed every sign of relief, for she had heard from Zepho that Adam had left to look for the two Priests. Inside the long Service Corridor, there was chaos in spite of valiant efforts by the village Masters, as over five hundred people, hundreds of animals and piles of possessions tried to settle down. The noise was indescribable and the mood, that of anxiety at the unfamiliar and, excitement at the future possibilities.

A second corridor now opened up running round from Clearance to School House, in the reverse direction to the first corridor. There was now a corridor right around the world at School End and gave the Valhalla's inhabitants and their possessions much more space. All the space now available only had to hold them during the landing. Once they were down on the surface of the planet, more accommodation would become available through the doors, which were at that moment, above their heads.

Instructions, on how to seal both the outer and inner doors of the Service Corridor, were to be found on the wall just inside the inner doors, although Adam felt certain that a different form of sealing would have been undertaken automatically, if they have failed to accomplish it manually.

Evening Star and Adam, leaving Companion with Adam's mother on the way, walked the full length of the two Corridors, giving assurances and restating what had already been explained to them regarding the vertical beds. By the time Adam reached the step to the Library of Light, he was totally exhausted and even the sight of the Master of Hope sitting smiling, failed to cheer him up.

"I'm glad to see you here, Sir" he said wearily. "Perhaps you would now take charge."

"No, you are in charge for the moment Adam. Your time has come and you have met the challenge well, young man. Only you can lead us into Paradise and once there, heal the wounds amongst us. You have, as the saying goes, lived to see the signs."

Grateful for these words, Adam smiled and placed his hand on the Master's shoulder. "The Pilot will get you there, with a little local help from me" he said "but you will have to help me when we arrive." He straightened up "In the meantime, I must get some rest." Adam turned and walked slowly up the steps into the Library. In spite of his outward confidence Adam was thinking of all the things that could go wrong. It worried him a great deal. Supposing the Valhalla Haven develops the problems that had beset Valhalla Jonah? Supposing the doors to the corridors had not been sealed properly? The more he thought about these and related matters, the more distressed he became. Evening Star tried her best to reassure him and point out there was little he could do about it away. Very soon, in spite of his worries and the noises, he was asleep with Evening Star standing over him.

Technically, the landing went smoothly enough. For the humans and animals inside the Valhalla Haven Service Corridor it was very frightening, in spite of their now almost unconscious state. The air was loaded with a drug that operated equally well on all forms of life. First there were some violent jolts, then after several periods of sideways force, what had up till then been the floor slowly became a wall and the wall with the beds slowly became the floor. Then for a brief period, the floor took on a slope which, the Pilot had warned them was the manoeuvring jets of the school end removing some of the artificial gravity (or spin) of the vessel. Just for a moment everyone found themselves floating almost weightlessly. This was very scary particularly for the adults but didn't last long enough to cause any major panic. Finally, with nearly everybody in a bed, as instructed, the force upon them became two or three times its normal strength. During this time the animals amongst them were remarkably well behaved, suffering the pressure with quiet dignity. This continued for about a quarter of an hour accompanied by several loud intermittent and indefinable noises. Then, without warning, after a roaring noise of terrific intensity, there was a large bump and a lurch and all became quiet and the pressure upon them returned to normal.

In the Library of Light, the chairs had rotated to allow for the different attitude of the room, and the second band of screens (which had been across the old ceiling) now came into use. Adam slept on, throughout this period. Evening Star, after ensuring that he was comfortable, left Adam and went to join her family. For the first time in their lives, men trod a truly flat floor between the beds in the Service Corridor, and the doors that had been in the original ceiling, opened to reveal further extensive space for living and animal accommodation. Fortunately, this area, the original commissioning engineer's accommodation, was now accessible from the Corridors. It proved spacious enough to house most of the pig, goat and chicken livestock, together with a multitude of personal pets. Along the walls set into the floor of the completely flat accommodation rooms were channels about a hands breadth deep and along which fresh water now flowed constantly. It very soon became clear that these channels were taking away any waste placed in them. The air in both corridor and accommodation areas was kept reasonably fresh by some unknown means. Drinking water came out of things which the Valhalla Pilot said were called taps which, to the amazement of all, you could turn on and off. Equally strange was the hidden lighting which came on for twelve hours, and then dimmed for a further twelve. The air temperature was kept pretty cool throughout their confinement, presumably to keep the smells to an absolute minimum.

Adam awoke, after a much needed rest, and made another quick tour of the corridors. "An utter shambles" he thought "is the best way to describe them. I will have to chivvy the village elders and the Priesthood into restoring some kind of order."

He consulted Star. "Those farmers and villagers" she informed him "who thought the signs were not indicative of the coming of the end of the World are in a state of shock and disinclined to do anything. Those who believed it was to be the end, are finding it difficult to do very much, except hang onto their possessions and eat and sleep."

It took a long time to get the elders and Priesthood representatives together, but eventually they were briefed by Adam as to what was going to happen in the coming week and what part they were expected to play.

The week that followed the landing was, perhaps, the worst time of all. People were in neither their old World nor the New. For many, the day had a dreamlike quality which, afterwards, could only be vaguely recollected. Adam's only subsequent memory was of his answering interminable questions, and of settling inevitable disputes. Each morning, when the lights in the Corridor brightened, a long queue of people would form outside the Library of Light wanting help of one kind or another. Evening Star would let these people through in ones or twos.

"Next" would shout Adam, and wait for the person to come forward. "What's the problem?" he would ask.

"My wife's about to have a baby. Can some privacy be arranged for her?"

"Not very much I'm afraid" replied Adam. "You'll have to build up your luggage to form partitions for the moment." He thought for a moment, and then turned to Evening Star, "We are bound to have births and deaths before we are moved to Paradise" he said "Ask the Master of Hail if we can allocate one of the rooms in the new living space for this purpose." Adam turned back to the man before him,

"Give my best wishes to your wife, and good luck."

"Next" he shouted. A fat woman approached him.

"All the children in my section of the Corridor have running noses and complain of feeling unwell. What should we do?"

"Nothing" reassured Adam. "We are all likely to have mild symptoms of illnesses we have never before experienced. It's part of the procedure to protect us from serious diseases, which will be encountered in our New World. Next!" Two men entered eyeing each other aggressively. One of them spoke.

"Kadesh here, has stolen one of my chickens" he insisted.

"you're a liar, Caleb" shouted Kadesh. "You've lost it, don't know where it is, and have decided to blame me for it. Just because I own more chickens than you do."

"No you don't"

"Yes I do. Go find your own chickens!"

Adam held his hand up. "Listen both of you, but Caleb in particular. Was this missing chicken confined in a cage or attached by leash to anything?"

"No" admitted Caleb, "But I'd know it anywhere and I've seen it in amongst Kadesh's chickens."

"Go, both of you" said Adam slowly, "and remind yourselves of the fifth Commandment written in the pillar." He turned to Evening Star again, "Get these two out of here. They're wasting my time with things they should be able to resolve by themselves.

"Next" The two men were replaced by a clearly worried girl.

"I should have gone to Clearance today because I'm fifteen." She said shyly. "Where should I go now?"

Adam had once before put that question to the Valhalla Pilot, but he put it again to be absolutely sure. The girl waited patiently and watched with amazement as Adam spoke to an apparently invisible being, whose voice was so clear and precise and appeared to possess vastly superior knowledge. Soon, Adam turned to the girl and grinned.

"You can let it be known that no one will ever have to go through 'Clearance' again. Something has been done to us over the last few days. Checks are not necessary any more."

With a whoop of joy, the girl departed.

And so it would continue all day and every day, questions, complaints, disputes, reassurances and yet more questions. The provision of this indispensable service, to a worried and restless population, elevated Adam's status in their eyes considerably. So far as Adam himself was concerned, it kept him fully occupied, and gave him a deeper appreciation of the complexity of the life support and other mechanisms hidden behind the locked doors now above their heads.

Chapter Seventeen – The Planet, Paradise

Throughout the week after landing, and in spite of the appalling smells created by the animals, the air in the Corridor and associated rooms remained comparatively fresh. People gradually began to feel less helpless and tired, as the effects of the drugged water supply wore off. Clear, uncontaminated water was available which had a very different, sharper, taste to that which had been previously available in the Valhalla Haven. In the Library of Light, Adam tried contacting the 'Ghost' World but the communications facility was inoperative. The Pilot said this facility was no longer necessary as they would shortly be meeting the inhabitants of the other vessels face to face.

Finally, the day came when the Valhalla Pilot announced that a party could leave. Apart from sheer curiosity, hunger drove them into exploration. The purpose of the bars along the passage through the book Library, and along the wall of School House now became clear. For the humans, they provided a ladder up to the outer circular door.

For the first glimpse of their new World, Adam chose a mixed party of men and women, about ten in number, and left detailed instructions as to what to do in event of their not returning. As he wrestled with the lock above his head, Adam was surprised that he felt no fear, only excitement in anticipation of what he would see. In the event, it turned out to be a bit of an anticlimax. Adam and two of the men heaved the lock door open and Adam climbed out onto the flat side wall of School House which stood about three strides above the now horizontal end of the Valhalla Haven. He took a deep breath and almost choked on the freshness of the air. It stung his lungs and made his head spin for several moments. He found himself standing at the edge of a huge circular disk that had once been School End of the Valhalla Haven. It was reasonably warm, but it was night time. He would have been able to see very little, were it not for the fact that the Valhalla Haven's sun still shone gently from the point above the centre of the World's End. Peering the other way out into the dark, he could see what looked like a field of green corn shoots stretching away into the distance. Of the rest of Valhalla Haven there was no sign. There were still one or two lumps where the wildmen had once lived, but no fields, no ridges, no villages, no Bell End by the look of it. All Adam could see upwards, were swirling dark masses of something at an indeterminate height.

All of a sudden, there swept over Adam an immense wave of relief. Until that moment he hadn't realised just how tense and anxious he had been over the past two weeks. This emotion was closely followed by a surge of joy and excitement. They had made it. Whoopee! Adam could have danced in his moment of triumph. He felt almost drunk and carefree. He did a little jig until he spotted one of the other men looking at him rather strangely. This sobered him up and brought him back to the present.

Adam got down on his knees, and looked over the edge of School End more closely. It dawned on him that, what he had thought was corn, were really the tops of more trees that he had ever seen in his life. This revelation enabled him to estimate the distance to the ground. A shout from one of the women behind him, made him look in the direction she was pointing. Way out in the dark, shone another bright light, at the centre of another dark disk. Then the women picked out another light, and another, until at least six had been positively identified. The peculiar thing was that they all seemed to be of different sizes, and it took the party quite a while to arrive at the logical conclusion that, either all the Valhallas had been different sizes, or that each vessel lay much further away from them, than anything had ever been before.

They had landed in a natural clearing in a forest but, even so, the most alarming aspect of this first venture 'outside', was the speed with which the air moved over the surface of this World. Adam was nearly blown off his feet at the first strong gust. Wind was very rare in the World from which they had come.

When everyone had had a good look, the party went below and a second group was allowed up. This procedure continued all night, for many people still had to be convinced that the Valhalla Haven was no more. Soon there were parties with a strong rope, made up from animal tethers tied together; asking permission to lower themselves into the trees to explore for food, which was getting very short. After a visit to where the lumps had once been, and where the covering on the new and different tools had already started to dissolve, parties were allowed to leave on the understanding that they didn't leave sight of the Central Sun, and that they reported anything unusual or beneficial to the population as a whole.

In spite of his hunger, Adam left the organisation of these parties to the Village Masters, and went to the Library of Light to speak with the Pilot. There were no horizontal steps now into the Library and he had to walk on the mosaic wall. He didn't ask the sort of questions that, on reflection, he would have more properly needed to know such as, was the planet safe, was the surface firm, were there any other humans already on the planet. Adam asked about the things he saw immediately about him, and once again received answers that he didn't altogether expect.

When he'd finished asking about the wind, the clouds, the trees, etc. he asked about the other, one time, Ghost Worlds.

"Have all the vessels landed now?"

"No. The Valhalla Jonah has not landed."

"How many vessels have landed near here?"

"Eight vessels."

"And the Valhalla Queen, has she landed?"

"The whole of the Valhalla Queen has landed in deep water a long way from the Valhalla Haven."

"And when will the Valhalla Jonah land?"

"She will never land" said the Pilot briefly.

Adam was non-plussed. "Is she not meant to land?"

"Yes, but she has disintegrated" was the reply.

Adam was horrified. "Why? …. I mean what has happened to the Valhalla Jonah?"

At that point Evening Star, and Fathers Zepho and Heman slipped into seats beside him to hear what the Pilot had to say.

"Valhalla Jonah's control circuits were faulty and she failed …"

"Excuse me for interrupting" said Adam who by experience had found the Pilot stopped and listened if you interposed a question. "Excuse me, but could you either keep the description very simple or show us visually what happened?"

On the screen, in front of each of the watchers, appeared a crescent shape taking up a quarter of the view. It was, explained the Pilot, a view of the fourth planet in the system as seen from the Valhalla Inn's telescope. In the foreground was a shape the watchers had not seen before, but which the Pilot identified as an external view of the Valhalla Jonah. Through Adam's mind immediately there flashed the words of the chant 'Tall men marching' for, with the telescope mounted at one end like a head and landing legs at the back, the Valhalla Jonah looked like a man with a long body and short legs. At first, nothing seemed to be happening, but then the watchers noticed two things. The Valhalla Jonah was rotating slowly about its long axis and also was slowly dwindling in size. Very smoothly but with inexorable progress, the Valhalla Jonah was moving straight for the planet behind. As it shrank to microscopic proportions the Pilot explained.

> "The controls to the Valhalla Jonah's engines have been faulty almost from the start of the expedition but the extent of the malfunctions only made themselves known a few days ago by which time the ten Valhalla vessels were approaching the solar system just below the planetary plane. The Valhalla Jonah failed to respond to redirection and found itself on a collision course with a minor planet which circles about 250 million miles from the central sun. It was a one in eight million chance."

By this time the Valhalla Jonah had dwindled to a dot.

> "What you are now seeing actually happened twelve days ago. I must warn you that there will be a brilliant flash when the vessel strikes the planet."

Adam marvelled at the cool detached way the Valhalla Haven Pilot could describe the destruction of its sister World.

The watchers sat in silence as the dot vanished and the planet floated serenely on the screen. Suddenly, there was a white stab of light on the dark side of the planet, which swiftly dimmed in brightness, but expanded in size until it enveloped an area about a quarter of the size of the crescent.

"It was a small dwarf planet" continued the Pilot.

The first indication that something was wrong with the planet was when the smooth outline of its crescent became irregular. Then a vast cloud, expanding slowly outwards from the point of impact, obscured all further developments.

"The planet has broken up into millions of separate pieces. It was not anticipated that the vessel's neutron bombs would ever have to deal with so large an object, and they had set themselves at maximum detonation. Anything smaller would have been completely vaporised as was the intention."

"Why" said Evening Star recovering from the shock of what they had just seen, "why should any vessel want to vaporise anything, and what does vaporise mean exactly?"

"Each vessel was equipped with an engine that would, in the last resort, explode and reduce to a gas any stray matter with which it might collide. This increasing the chances of survival for the following vessels" replied the Pilot.

"What has happened to the planet now?" asked Zepho.

"It will continue to circle the central sun but in the form of millions of fragments. It is unfortunate for it will create a hazard for future space travel in the region."

"It was also unfortunate for Naomi and the other people in the Valhalla Jonah" said Adam tersely. "Poor old Jonah." Adam was horrified by the apparent indifference of the Pilot. After all, it might have happened to the Valhalla Haven. It was always a shock to be reminded that the Pilot was not a human being. In silence he rose and, with Evening Star, climbed the bar ladder onto the flat surface of the School End.

Outside, it was beginning to get light, the wind had dropped and the clouds thinned out. As it became lighter, the several hundred men, women and children present watched spellbound as the vista extended before them. The vessels had landed in a wide valley partly covered with trees. Low hills could be seen in the distance. Through the valley ran a river, which had lately carved a gorge for itself about thirty strides in depth. One thing that nothing could have adequately prepared them for was the sight of their first sunrise. Everyone watched with utter amazement as the brilliant orb of the planet's sun rose over the trees. It was much larger and brighter that they were used to seeing in the Valhalla Haven. Later in the day it became much hotter as well, for that first day was an almost cloudless one. Furthermore, a sun that shone with a constant intensity, but which moved across the sky, and disappeared at night was going to take a lot of getting use to.

The most striking features of the vista were those of colours, sounds and smells. Nowhere in the Valhalla Haven had there been such rich and contrasting greens and browns. The blue of the sky and pure white of the clouds were quite outside human experience. Equally amazing for everyone were the sounds of wind in the trees, running water in the streams and rivers, and unaccountable animal noises. The first smells they encountered, though strange, were less powerful then those they were used to in the Valhalla Haven. This new World was clearly going to provide them with a greater breadth of experience than they could ever have imagined possible.

Just then, a sound of excited voices floated up from the ground just below School House. Adam went to the edge and, looking down, saw some men dragging a dead four legged animal through the trees. "It didn't take us long to catch this" shouted up one of the wildmen. "Send down a fire stone and some oil and we'll soon have it cooked." Then in response to further questioning he added, "This bow, together with these arrows, worked a treat. My brother, Manahath, got this creature with his second shot. Now we have plenty of wood, down here, it should be easy enough to make many more arrows in no time at all."

Adam smiled to himself and squeezed Evening Star's hand. "Everything is going to be alright" he said. But to himself he thought "just so long as they don't start shooting those arrows at each other."

"I don't know about alright" said a farmer standing near him. "It's all very well for hunting, but how can I plant things in amongst all these trees. Why, even the shadows don't remain still in this World!"

Adam laughed "If that's the only problem we have, it won't be so bad a place to live. My main concern is how hot and cold it's going to get."

That evening, the sky was clear and, for the first time, everyone saw the great vault of the sky darken and the stars come out. Up until then the word star had only been used as a girl's name, and to describe the shape of the marks on the outer casing of the two airlocks, 'M' lock and 'O' lock. Now, the Pilot informed Adam of a third, and original meaning, when they asked it to explain the little points of light in the sky.

It was Alvan, the Master of Hope Village that was, who first suggested a trip to meet up with the folk from the other Valhallas. A small group of volunteers went with him. Some of the group were farmers, on the look out for more fertile and less densely wooded land. Some were wildmen, looking for a strip nearer the river where they could settle by themselves. Alvan went to establish formal contact with who ever was in charge of the other human groups. It was soon discovered that events, leading up to and during the landing, in the other Valhallas had been much more chaotic than in the Valhalla Haven. Most of the groups looked completely lost and quite leaderless. It became a relatively simple matter to persuade these groups that some form of over-all authority was essential, and that all of humanity should pool its resources for the time being.

There was tremendous excitement when each of the Valhalla's saw the other Valhalla's animal life. Although the creatures had been described verbally between the worlds, it was quite something else for the Valhalla Haven's and Inn's population to see a cow or a lamb for the first time. Likewise the Valhalla King, Light, Moss and Night's population were eager to see what goats and pigs looked like in the flesh. All of them wanted to see the bird life from the Valhalla Over and Pass, but most of it flew off as soon as it was released, to mingle with the bird life native to the planet.

Over the following weeks and, in spite of considerable trepidation, it wasn't long before most of the human and animal population moved out of the eight Valhalla Vessels, and took up residence along the river bank. Food was plentiful, and those that suffered too severely from a fear of open spaces, went to live in the caves that dotted the cliffs of the gorge nearby. All the books in the Valhalla Libraries were taken out and stored. Half a year after the 'landing', most of the people still lived quite close to the 'vessels', but there was talk of moving off to follow the game herds. No other exactly similar human life was encountered, although occasionally, tribes of small creatures that stood erect, were seen. These tribes also lived by hunting, but seemed ignorant of fire and had only very basic tools of any kind.

Soon the Valhalla vessels lay deserted, and after a period of a year the artificial suns, having performed their tasks to perfection, ceased to function. Young trees started growing right up against the Vessel's superstructure, and ivy began to climb and cover the stubby legs.

One day, about a year and a half after the 'landing', Master Adam, as he was now called, left the cave from where he governed the nearby fast growing village, and walked back through the woods to the Valhalla Haven. He was now happily married, and was generally acknowledged to be the leader of the whole human community. All manor of changes had occurred by then, some geographical, some sociological. Most of the wildmen, some one hundred and fifty strong and being a gathering of all nine Valhalla's misfits had headed up river to seek out their own lands (much to the relief of many people.) The Priesthood which had been few in number on the other Valhalla's congregated with Geuel and his followers just outside the main village protective fence. They aimed to build an enclosure of their own.

Adam was now undertaking a trip he had meant to take for some time, but the pressure of everyday events had forced him to postpone. Swinging his fur cape aside, now worn both for warmth and for status, he climbed the long wooden ladder which lay up the side of the Valhalla Haven. Entering the School House, he made his way down into the Library of Light. There, everything was as it had been before, and Adam settled into a chair and called up the 'interrogation' programme.

"Pilot, I am here probably for the last time. We are now settled on this planet, and I imagine your task is done. But before I put the past completely from my mind, I would like to know more of the reasons for our journey here. If we are but part of a greater plan, it has been forgotten thousands of years ago. If we have some part to play in the future, I would like to know when that will be. Will we remain here for a year, a hundred years, or, as in the Valhalla Haven, for thousands of years? Who was the Master Builder, and what was his grand design? How long will you remain here for advice and possible shelter, in times of trouble? You see there are many questions and, as usual, I don't know whether I will understand all the answers." Adam stopped and waited. After a few moments, a new and unfamiliar voice spoke.

"Good day to you friend. This is no longer the Pilot talking to you, but one of your own kind. I speak to you across a gulf of hundreds and perhaps thousands of years. This message has been recorded, and you will only be listening to it if you have landed and asked for information as to the purpose of your journey across space. I would make a bargain with you. I will trade information for information; answers for answers and news for news. Is this procedure acceptable to you?"

Adam nodded unconsciously, and then remembering that a verbal reply was required, said "It is acceptable."

The voice continued. "At the outset, one of us has to trust the other. I propose, therefore, to provide you with information in two parts. In the first place, I will recount the reasons for your journey. Then you will be asked to give an account of recent events and attitudes in the last days of your vessel, and the first days after landing. Finally, I shall provide you with advice for the future, since we have considerable experience of planetary colonisation, and the problems that arise." There was a pause and the voice went on.

"This first part will not be repeated indefinitely. If you wish others to hear it, they should be called now."

Adam pondered the matter carefully before replying. "I wish to hear it alone now and I am ready now, but I will bring a selection of men and women to hear the second part."

Chapter Eighteen – At The Beginning

Adam sat upright in complete silence for a few moments, waiting for the promised message. The lighting dimmed until he appeared to be seated in the centre of a void, with nothing above, below or on either side of him. At the onset of total blackness there appeared, on the walls of the spherical room, countless points of white light. Somehow Adam knew that they represented stars, although they were much more densely packed on the wall in front of him, than the view of them he had had looking up into the sky over the last year and a half.

Even as he watched, trying to pick out patterns amongst them, Adam noticed that the stars in front of him seemed to be slowly spreading out, whilst those behind him were closing in. Then, from the point where the stars were spreading, there formed the figure of a man, small at first but rapidly expanding to full size. This almost perfect three dimensional projection just allowed Adam enough time to notice the man's brief, but quite fantastic, clothing before it began to speak. The voice was deep and clear, coming it appeared, directly from the image.

"My name is Acternon Z5057818. My birthplace was the planet Zenon, which is the sixth planet circling the star Denos IV, which is located quite close to the central plane of this Galaxy. As psychologist at the Institute of Advanced Research, Implementation Department, I am one of the humans responsible for the construction of the space vehicle which for hundreds, and perhaps thousands of years you have regarded as being all of creation and your home.

My story covers only those facts which relate to your own recent tremendous journey and present situation. I have been as careful as I can, to stick to words and phrases which you will understand, or can look up in the Dictionary. My greatest fear is that your language, by now, has altered too drastically for the Master Computer to deal with the translation. In this matter, I can only hope that the programmers' routines were sufficiently sophisticated. I have throughout, referred to years as being the units of time with which you are familiar, for example, the length of time between similar crop growing seasons in your recent world and, miles, of which you are not familiar, one mile being roughly the distance across your world. However, you must prepare yourself for my explanation to include some difficult concepts, and for magnitudes of distance and time far greater than those to which you are accustomed."

At this point, Acternon's image floated silently to one side, so that other images could appear beside him, representing the scenes and developments as he described them.

"This story has no finite beginning, for who knows when the human race first came to, or evolved within, this galaxy. I should explain that a Galaxy is the name given to the vast cluster of stars in which my Sun Denos IV, and your sun, are two particular members. Each and every other star in our Galaxy is also a sun, some larger and some smaller than our own, and the distances between stars are so great they are measured in light years – that is – the distance light can travel in a year.

Some five hundred years ago (from when I speak) the humans on the planets circling the stars nearer the Galactic centre had learnt how to travel outwards, colonising new planets as they went. But they grew ambitious, wishing to secure the long term future of the human race by travelling to another galaxy, and not just to other the stars in our own Galaxy. Now, just at this time, two smaller galaxies happened to be passing close to ours, and it was decided to organise an expedition to both.

After a twenty two year debate, the necessary funds were voted, and a Foundation set up to organise and implement a project of monumental proportions. There was to be an expedition mounted as soon as possible. At early meetings of the Foundation, it was agreed that vessels could be built to carry humans for up to about ten thousand years of journey time. But travel times of over a hundred thousand years, which is what would be necessary to reach the passing star 'clouds' or galaxies, would have to be tackled in an entirely different manner. I am no engineer, but I can imagine the problems of planning a space vessel that would be reliable enough in all its aspects, to carry a human cargo across the vast gulf of space between our galaxy and the nearby star 'clouds', for a journey length calculated to be at least 245, 000 years."

The descriptive images began again, beside Acternon, and gave Adam a very clear impression of the principles involved. "After many years of planning, a scheme has been devised which, in scale and imagination, dwarfs nearly all the other current projects at the Institute. The 'ship' chosen for the journey, will not be given any power of its own, mainly because its builders fear that the travellers might take control and break off the expedition, but will be accelerated and fired like an arrow from a bow. Although the analogy with a bow and arrow, is satisfactory for dealing with the technique, it is totally inadequate when dealing with the scale of the engineering involved.

For the 'ship' on which the star travellers will live for thousands of years, which has been named 'The Trinity City', comprises twelve planets orbiting a triple sun system. The 'bow', which will accelerate the stellar system to about three quarters the speed of light, will be 2,000 light years long, and the power to be used is that of the stars along the path of the expedition. I say 'will be' rather than 'was' because, as I speak this message to you, the Main expedition has not yet set off, for reasons that will become clear to you in a moment. Nor, probably, will it have done so when you listen to this message, because your journey is but part of the construction of the 'bow' I refer to.

Now the path along which the expedition is to be 'accelerated', if it is to be some 2,000 light years long, cannot be a single physical 'pathway' but must consist of magnetic beams, spaced at regular intervals along the way, drawing upon the power of the stars nearby. This conversion, from solar energy, into magnetic energy into kinetic energy – that is - the pull and push required for the Trinity City, called for immensely sophisticated machinery, positioned in such a configuration, that it will be lined up in the direction of the destination star 'clouds', at exactly the right time. This task alone, occupied a team of astronomers with computational assistance for many years. You, until recently, were part of the equipment convoy or caravan, along the path of the proposed expedition, to set up the magnetic field. You are now on a planet, within my Galaxy, in the path of one of the two Main Expeditions which are to travel to the nearby star 'clouds'.

Once it had been decided to set up the Trinity City 'Accelerator', it was agreed, for reasons of economy, to combine the equipment journey 'caravan' with the colonisation of planets along the path of the accelerator. By following the progress and ultimate development of these artificially implanted colonies, we could improve our knowledge of the Galactic periphery in the two particular directions."

And now Adam saw, for real, what he had already guessed whilst in the Valhalla Haven. Even so, he was not prepared for the grandeur and the beauty of the whole 'caravan' as seen from a long way off.

Acternon continued "So it came about that, for each of the two 'caravans', some 650 space vessels were assembled, in groups of ten, one group for each solar system which satisfied the dual conditions of, correct position as any energy source, and having planets capable of supporting life. The vessels were placed in relation to one another in the form of a spiral helix, for safety reasons, approximately 400 miles apart. A further twenty five scout, monitoring and defence vessels were added to accompany them, four of which are about eight hundred million miles ahead of the main group, and act as a vanguard.

Each space vessel is approximately two and a half miles long and one mile across, with telescope equipment at one end and an engine at the other. The engines not only provide power to accelerate, de-accelerate and manoeuvre the vessels, but are also programmed to provide heat for the human and animal occupants. The entire 'caravan' is planned to travel at about one hundred and forty million miles an hour – that is – 20% of the speed of light.

As a result it will take the last vessels in the Caravan ten thousand years to travel the whole two thousand light years necessary for the construction of the 'bow' for the main expedition.

When the 'caravan' is regarded from a distance, it looks like a gigantic spiral spring, with little beads upon it every four hundred miles or so, the whole length from vanguard to rearguard being somewhere in the region of one billion miles.

Within each group of ten vessels, detaching themselves from the main column about once every one hundred and fifty of your years, there has been built a certain amount of technical redundancy – that is – two or three similar pieces of equipment where one perfectly reliable system would have done. For example, the vessels which generate the impulse field for the Trinity City to follow, commonly referred to as 'field ships', need to be three in number, although five have been included (and what are called 'cloaked' to avoid discovery). Only one transmitter vessel, commonly called 'beacon' vessel, is actually required, etc. Although each vessel is the same diameter, the length varies according to the equipment carried. And included along with the equipment, but in a separate compartment, is the human and animal population. The first two vessels in each ten has animal life up to the size of pigs and dogs. The next five vessels are mainly pasture, and little agriculture, with room for some of the larger animals. The two transmitter or 'beacon' vessels have human and bird life and the tenth vessel contains marine life.

All vessels have human life, except the tenth one filled with water. We do not expect all the animal life to survive on your planet, unless the conditions are particularly favourable. It will depend on whether it can compete effectively against any life already on the planet.

Each vessel travels through the void facing backwards, i.e. engine pointing forward, after the initial acceleration to normal speed. Each vessel is rotating to give it an artificial gravity, making a complete turn about seventy times an hour. We have arranged for each group of ten vessels to be in radio communication with each other, in order that their language should not diverge too far since, one day, all the inhabitants will become a common pool of humanity on a single planet. The spin of the vessel and the length of the day, may be adjusted towards the end of the journey to allow you more quickly to adapt to the spin and length of the day on your new planet."

Adam was touched by just a twinge of homesickness, when pictures of the vessel's interior flashed across the screen.

"All service functions in each vessel, for example air purification, disease control, temperature, water quality, humidity, etc. etc., are completely automatic and sealed from all internal interference. There are two ways into or out of each vessel, when it is part of the convoy, which are controlled by voice locks. These locks are controlled by time clocks, in addition to the correct audio sentence-code being required. Thus the voice locks on the airlocks at the top of the two staircases, will not work under any circumstances, until the vessel is within the destination solar system, or in the case of major emergency. There is both an inner door and an outer door. The inner door has to be closed before the outer door can be opened, to prevent anyone emptying the air from your vessel out into the void. The voice locks into the Book Libraries, which were an afterthought in the design anyway, have a whole series of separate controlling devices.

Inside each vessel we had a number of physical problems, a number of social problems and few psychological problems. Although it was my task to deal with the psychological matters, I will try and outline the physical and social structure that was eventually devised."

Up to this time, Adam had only vaguely understood the meaning of Acternon's message. Now the story moved into much more familiar territory.

"Soil has been provided to a very considerable depth, between ridges that can accommodate periods of acceleration and de-acceleration, without massive earth movements occurring. Because of the angle at which the heat source of sun's rays strike the soil, the ridges have to be lower at the far end, and hence closer together at that end, to hold back the soil. The airlocks are high up to prevent them becoming blocked deliberately or accidentally, and also to permit less (but still some) centrifugal force, and hence weight, at the point of entry and exit to the vessel. The process used to maintain a satisfactory quality of genetic stock, commonly called 'Clearance', is necessary because of higher levels of radiation in space than are normally encountered on a planet. A small amount of genetic engineering has been necessary, to ensure that all humans will first go blind and subsequently die, if they are not 'vetted' for physical normality around their fifteenth year. 'Clearance' is also used as a device for controlling the size of population.

The village wells had, of course, to be at fixed locations within your vessel, so that clean water could be supplied to them. This meant that the villages also, for convenience, to be around each well. This allowed us to construct all the houses in the centre of each village, out of the same hard material as had been used to make Clearance, the School House and the housing near the lumps. This ensured that, however severe the fighting in your vessel, there would always be some dwellings left standing for the survivors. No doubt make-shift housing will also appear at the village edges when their populations becomes excessive.

A limiting factor for population growth is necessary for social as well as physical reasons. The same effect is applied, although it takes rather longer to make itself felt, by adjusting the temperature and humidity of the vessel's interior, which in turn controls the food supply allowing the size of the population to be 'adjusted' around subsistence level. This may sound very indifferent and cruel of us, but it is the only way to ensure that some of the population survives, for upwards of ten thousand years, in such a confined space. Incidentally, we have arranged for the crops to be more abundant than normal just before de-acceleration to compensate for the rather poorer crops when the engines will be full on and the sun's heat less. This may give rise to social problems since there will then be population with spare time on their hands."

Adam smiled wryly at this remark.

"At this moment in time, some two hundred years after the caravan has set forth, all the vessels seem to be functioning as planned, although three didn't come up to specification and had to be left behind. In addition Alpha Crystal and Valhalla Jonah have had some minor troubles. Even as I dictate this message the engineers in each vessel are topping up the lakes, for the water is used as fuel by the engines, and are sealing the voice locks in preparation for departure, having monitored performances to ensure that everything is functioning satisfactorily.

We do not know, how the structure of your society will alter over the coming centuries. This is something we, very much, want to know from you. For example, we arranged for housing on the lake island, where the implement store exists, as a place of refuge for mutants who, though surviving Clearance because their disfigurement was not hereditary, are likely to be spurned by society. Misfits may well also congregate there, and we would be interested in the success of this approach. Nor do we know how long the inhabitants of each World will remember their origins. We do not think it will be very long before the Beginning will just be a legend, and we bolstered that belief by introducing some books into the Library which described it as just that. One idea, I myself put forward and was accepted by our committee, was to provide plenty of clues about the past for the observant. We have made sure the children's lore and games, which have grown naturally over the past two hundred years, have developed with accurate facts imbedded in them. However, we did not deem it wise to allow the population of each vessel to conceive of an outside to their World. The whole truth would have been too unsettling, and would bring no advantage.

One of the greatest difficulties was to decide what level of learning would be reached during the voyage, both in the sense of the lowest and highest level of attainment. Should libraries be included and, if so, what should they contain? Would they not get destroyed over the years? Was there any point in educating the inhabitants, when most of the practical uses of that education would forever be beyond them? The result, as you now know, was a two tier library system, and it would be useful to know how this worked out in reality. The two library 'doors' are an advanced piece of technology, which even we can only create on a limited scale.

Of what has happened, between the time at which I speak, and the time at which you are listening to me, I can only tell you a small fraction. What I can 'foretell' is that some two years ago, your vessel commenced its de-acceleration, as the Scout Monitoring vessels detected a suitable solar system for you. At first, ten vessels of which yours was one, detached themselves from the rear of the main column. Then they shifted their axis of rotation through 90 degrees with the use of subsiduary engines on the vessel's periphery and then fired their main engines. This put them on course for the chosen system. Next, the vessels again realigned their engines to be facing the direction of travel, and started to slow them down. On reaching the outer planet of the destination system, both of the communications vessels split into two, and the machinery halves went into orbit around the outer planet, whilst the halves with life continued inwards.

The 'field' vessels were next to break up, and the machinery went into orbit near the central or largest Sun. The rest you know yourselves, although it may have seemed strange to you that, after such a tremendous journey, there was no possibility of landing the vessel intact. The landing of Engine and Service Corridor only, was arranged partly for psychological reasons, but also to allow for some practical snags. For example, once the spin of the vessel is removed, the soil will no longer hold its place. As regards psychological reasons, I decided that something fairly drastic was going to be necessary, to drive the inhabitants of each vessel out on to the surface of the destination planet. Having left their old homes up in the sky, I felt sure their links with the ship would be weakened, and that hunger would soon complete the task for me.

During the landing, you occupied one of the two Corridors which link the Rooms which house the Service monitoring equipment, and the Service Engineers accommodation. The corridors, which stretch right round the periphery of each vessel, have been equipped with de-acceleration couches. When your vessel approached the chosen planet you felt the changes brought about by the vessel going into orbit. Whilst a suitable landing spot or spots were being selected, you will have heard a series of loud noises, as the end of your world with the sun and service corridors was disconnected from the rest of the vessel. Then part of the spin was taken off your vessel the rest remaining so the whole unit could be brought down in a controlled manner. Finally, just before the touch down or landing, you would have heard the main engines working harder to break the speed of the vessel as it plunged through the atmosphere. Your recent week of confinement, before being allowed onto your planet, was to allow a modest degree of inoculation against diseases, and also to permit radiation treatment, thereby eliminating any future need of 'Clearance' procedures.

The remainder of your vessel, with the telescope on the front end, will continue to orbit your planet for two hundred years. The telescope should still be in full working order, and can be used via the control room in which you are now seated, during that time. After that, the part of your vessel still in orbit, together with the Engine and Control room unit on the ground, will be destroyed." Adam made a mental note to tell Zepho about this.

Acternon continued, "You have probably guessed by now, that we intended that you should remain on your planet indefinitely. Your journey through space is over, but a fuller life is only just beginning.

What about the Main Expedition, I can almost hear you saying? Well, that will pass your planet sometime in the future, but quite when I cannot say for it depends which vessel you are in, as this message has been incorporated into the memory banks of all the vessels. It will be quite a sight, I think as the 'Trinity City', travelling at 80% the speed of light, when fully up to speed, moves across your heavens. This expedition is the only chance we have of reaching the passing Star 'cloud'. These 'clouds' are not destined ever to combine with our Galaxy, they are going too fast to be able to do that. After the passing of the Expedition, there will be no equipment left permanently within your solar system, with the exception of the 'beacon' vessels orbiting the outer planet. That, your race may one day find, when all the rest of this history is forgotten or has become legend."

"Now, citizen or citizens of the future. I have kept my part of the bargain. Tell me everything you can remember about the journey, avoiding hearsay whenever possible. We would also be much obliged, if you could add a few words about your latest plans on the New World. Speak slowly and clearly, starting whenever you like during the next hour."

Three and a half hours later, Adam had finished his account and he felt exhausted. Slowly the lights came back on. How the Master Computer knew he hadn't dictated nonsense he didn't know. He had told everything he could remember. A lot of things fitted together as he had talked. The intention of the commandments; the presence of the wildmen; the need for the lumps; why only the Valhalla Haven had a Hall of Silence, being the first of the group of ten vessels; the purpose of the legends set out in the teachings and the lore books, and many other features.

Then he went to fetch the others, who would benefit from advice regarding planet colonisation. Adam chose a selection of men and women to join him from each of Valhalla colonies. There were only twelve seats in the Library of Light, but they managed to squeeze twenty four people into the room. Two from each colony were invited making eighteen in all. To this number were added Adam, Wildmen Bihan and Dishon (who had remained in the village), Kenaz and Zepho from the Priesthood and Evening Star. When Acternon had given his advice, they all with the exception of Adam left, talking excitedly amongst themselves. Adam was the last to leave the Library and before departing he turned and took a final look at the blank screen. He had grown quite fond of the Valhalla Pilot, and was sorry to be leaving. "Goodbye, Pilot."

"Thank you" he added, not expecting any answer, for he was not seated in the chair.

"Goodbye" replied the Pilot, with no hint of the emotion that Adam felt.

"Well, well" thought Adam, "so it has been listening to every word. Never mind. I wonder if the Pilot has made a note of it, and whether anyone, or how anyone, will ever listen to it!"

As Adam tramped through the trees reflecting on what he had heard from Acternon, the information he had given, in return, was winging its way at the speed of light towards the Transmitter Beacons twenty light hours away, orbiting the outer planet of their system.

"One day" he thought, "The Trinity City will appear in the sky. Will any of my race be here to wish them luck, and will they know the part their ancestors played? I hope so." For an instant, Adam had a vision of thousands of people staring up into the sky, wondering why a group of three stars should suddenly move in relation to all the other stars. Then he realised that this event would occur in hundreds and possibly thousands of years time, and would be so rapid that, more than likely, it would escape notice. And even if it was observed, its meaning would have been forgotten.

"Somehow", Adam resolved, "I must see that the history of our landing and tragic loss of Valhalla Jonah passes into the lore, and eventual legends, of our race. That presents me with a nice problem. Hm, perhaps I could invent a story, with a mixture of both fact and fiction, that describes the creation of the planet and the beginnings of the human race upon it. I could make it easier for our children to accept, than a story about travelling between stars and Galactic Expeditions"

Gradually his thoughts turned to his present surroundings, the trees, the path, the glow of a fire in the distance, supper and comradeship. "I shan't go back" he thought "I must put the Valhalla Haven out of my mind and start to think seriously about the future."

Adam came out of the woods and into a clearing in front of a cave, where he could see Companion lying asleep, and Evening Star directing the cooking of their supper. She was positively glowing with health as only a pregnant woman can.

"I still have a great deal to learn from Alvan and Zepho" He thought "from Alvan I have to pick up the skills of leadership, and how to get people to do what I want them to do and yet to think they thought of it themselves. And from Zepho, who is running the new school we have set up, I can learn about the best methods of teaching and what we should be teaching them." Adam continued to contemplate the group before him. There was quite a large party sitting down, with them, to have a meal that night. Alvan and his wife, had been invited to stay on after the trip to the Valhalla Haven, along with his old teacher Zepho. What with Adam's mother, his two brothers, his wife's mother, father and two brothers, there were twelve people in all.

"I must remember" Adam reminded himself , "to stop calling Zehpo 'Father', some of our old habits are hard to break but I've got to set the example." Recently, Alvan had agreed to drop the title of Hope Master and everyone now called him Alvan to his face. Similarly Father Zepho was now addressed as Zepho. At about the same time everyone had got into the habit of shortening Evening Star to Eve. Then Adam's thoughts were interrupted by a call for his attention.

"Adam, come and sit next to your mother" said Eve, patting the seat next to Miriam.

EPILOGUE

First Voice	"Is that all?"
Second Voice	"No, that's not all by a very long way, but it's enough to be going on with."
First Voice	"I think I knew that humans were once made out of solid matter, but it must have been very unpleasant to live such vulnerable and short lives."
Second Voice	"I agree, and that is why we changed to our present form."
First Voice	"I like the story, so far, but it was awful when the Valhalla Jonah, and Naomi, were destroyed. And it was sad when Adam said goodbye to the Pilot."
Second Voice	"Yes, the fate of the Valhalla Jonah was terrible, wasn't it. As far as the pilot was concerned, I think Adam had grown rather attached to it. But I believe Adam never did go back, nor did Eve. Zepho did return from time to time for information and for a special role he had been given by the pilot about which he said nothing to anyone."
First Voice	"What happens next in the story?"
Second Voice	"The next part deals with the descendants of the Valhalla Haven and her sister ships on the same planet 120,000 years later, and what has happened, in the meantime, to Trinity City,
First Voice	"Had the people changed much over that stretch of time?"
Second Voice	"Not much, as you will see. However, their technology was progressing. They had, by then, found nine of the major planets circling their Star or Sun."
First Voice	"Let me see, the Pilot said there were twelve major planets. That must mean they still had three to find. Why were these three planets difficult to see?"
Second Voice	"They were a long way out from the sun."
First Voice	"I see. When did the Main Expedition set off? And did they have any problems on the way to our Galaxy?"
Second Voice	"One day, perhaps, I'll tell you."

APPENDICES

Names of Characters Appendix I

Young citizens of the Valhalla Haven without title:

Adam	son of Ammiel and Miriam
Zilpah	wildgirl and wife of Cheran
Star (Evening Star)	daughter of Geuel
Naomi	girl in the Valhalla Jonah
Kenan	brother to Adam
Jabal	brother to Adam
Cain	a school friend of Adam
Abel	brother to Star
Enosh	brother to Star

The Master of Hope Village:	Alvan	His Deputy: Ebal
The Master of Hail Village	Lotan	His Deputy: Hemdan
The Master of Happy Village	Cheran	His Deputy: Ezer
The Master of Happen Village	Akan	His Deputy: Zoavan
The Master of Harp Village	Aran	His Deputy: Uz

The Patriarch	Eliphaz
The Deputy	Father Reuel
The Teacher Priest	Father Zepho
Two Priests at meeting	Father Zeush and Father Korah
Tall Priest	Father Jaalam

Priest of Hall of Voices	Father Kenaz
Priest of Clearance	Father Omar
2nd Teacher Priest	Father Jeush
3rd Teacher Priest	Father Gatam
4th Teacher Priest	Father Teman
Devotee of Eliphaz	Father Nahath
Medical Priest	Father Zerah
Medical Priest	Father Shammah
Bell Ringer	Javan
Legal Priest	Father Mizzah
Historian and Archivist	Father Heman
Runner Leader	Shepho
Scribe	Gether
Leader of Wildmen	Inga
Deputy Wildman	Bilhan
Wildman 1	Ithran
Wildman 2	Eshban
Wildman 3	Hori
Wildman 4	Onam
Wildman 5	Manahath
Wildman 6	Dishon
Wildman 7	Anah
Wildman 8	Zibeon (the flail)
Wildman 9	Shobal

Farmers	Ammiel (wife Miriam) (Adam's parents)
	Geuel (wife Rachel) (Star's parents)
	Gemalli
	Kadesh
	Eshcol
	Simon
	Anak
	Caleb
Villagers	Noah
	Kemual
	Shem
Retainers, Guards, etc.	Jacob
	Reuben
	Judah
	Zebulum
The Bully in Happen Hamlet	Shepho
Aunt and Uncle to Star	Mirriam and Reuben

APPENDIX 2

THE VALHALLA HAVEN

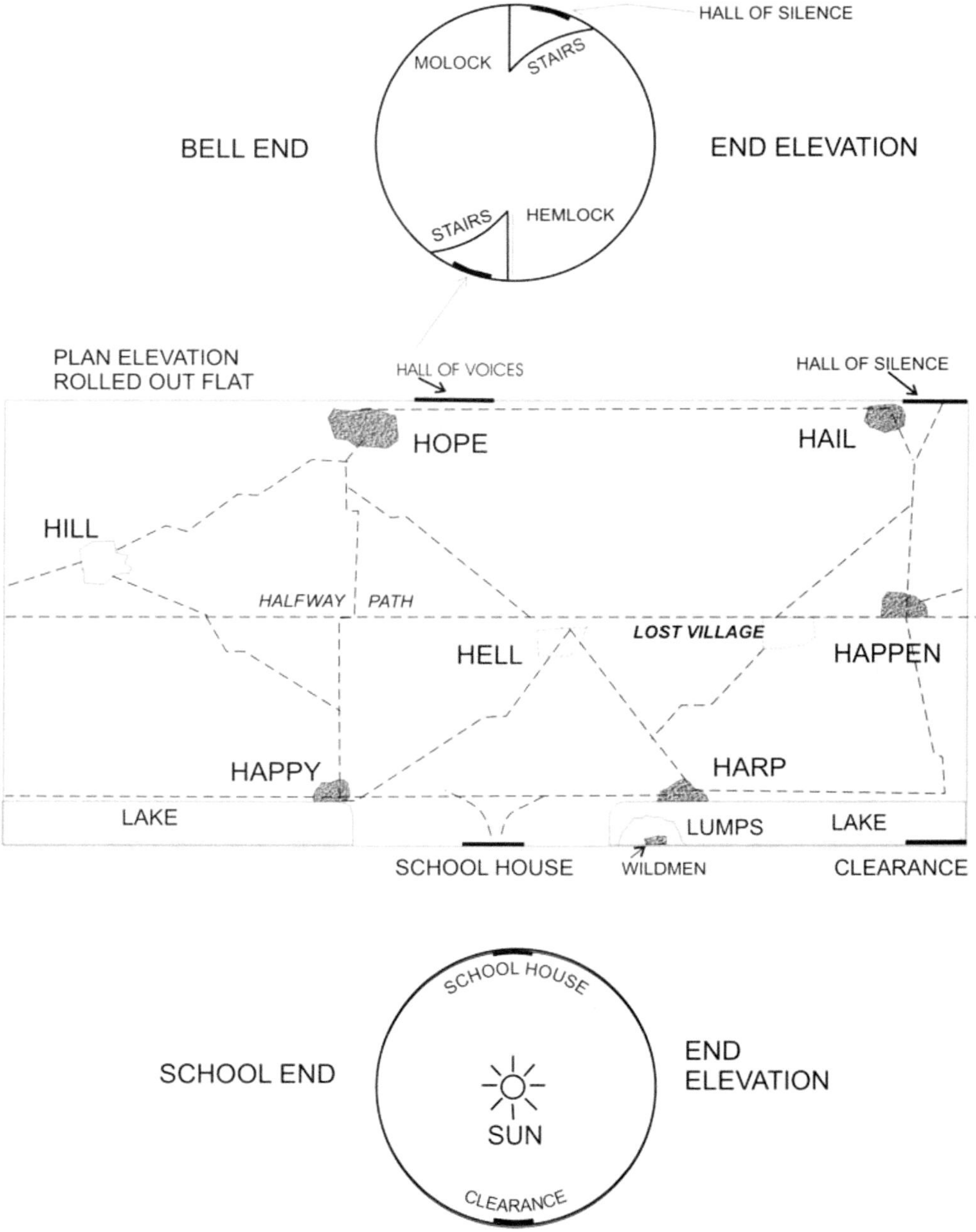

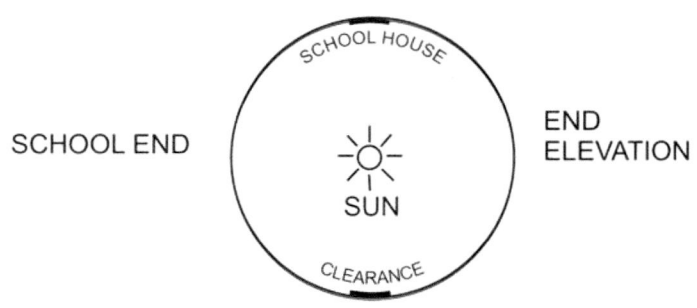

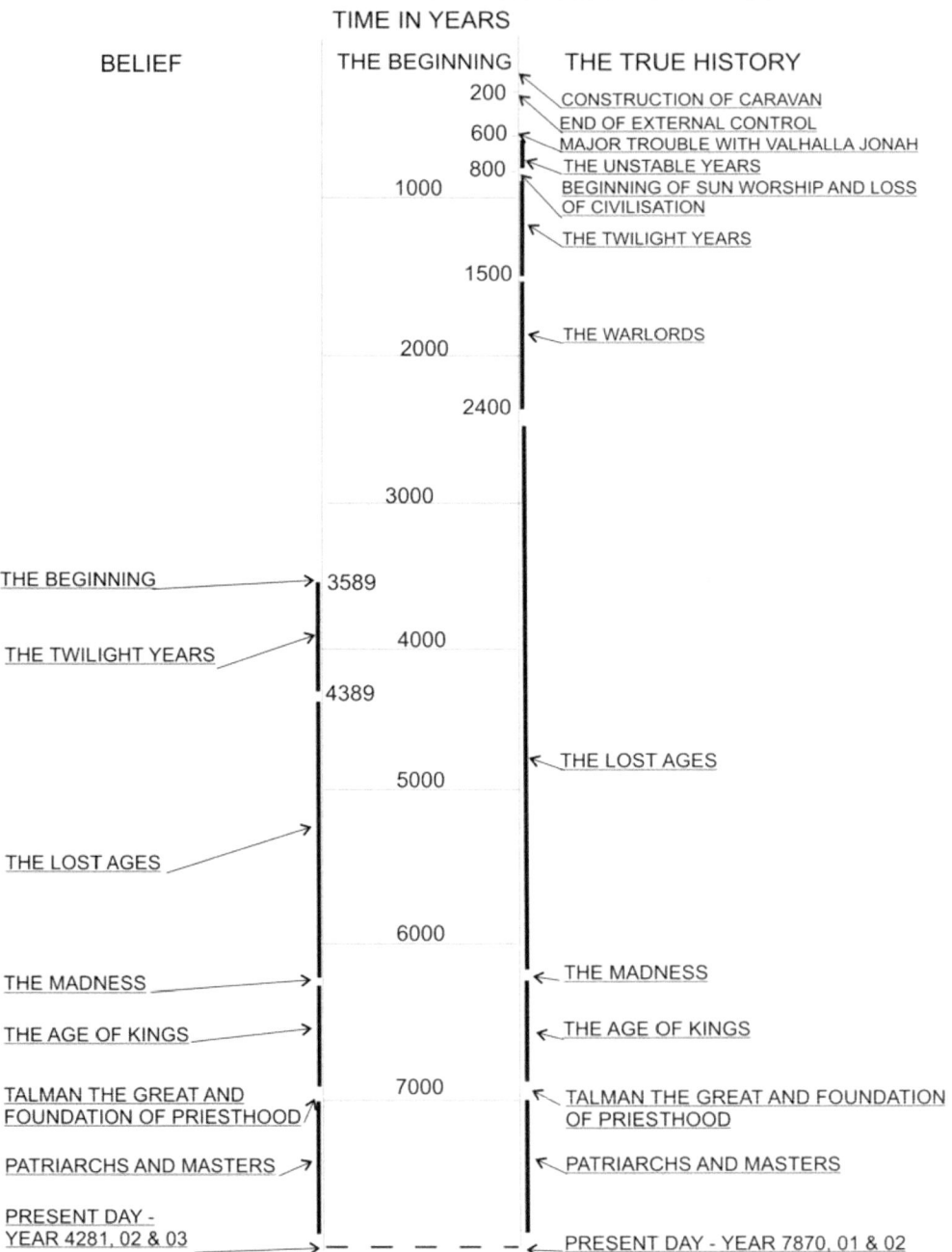

APPENDIX 4

CHRONOLOGY OF EVENTS DURING THE LAST YEARS IN THE VALHALLA HAVEN

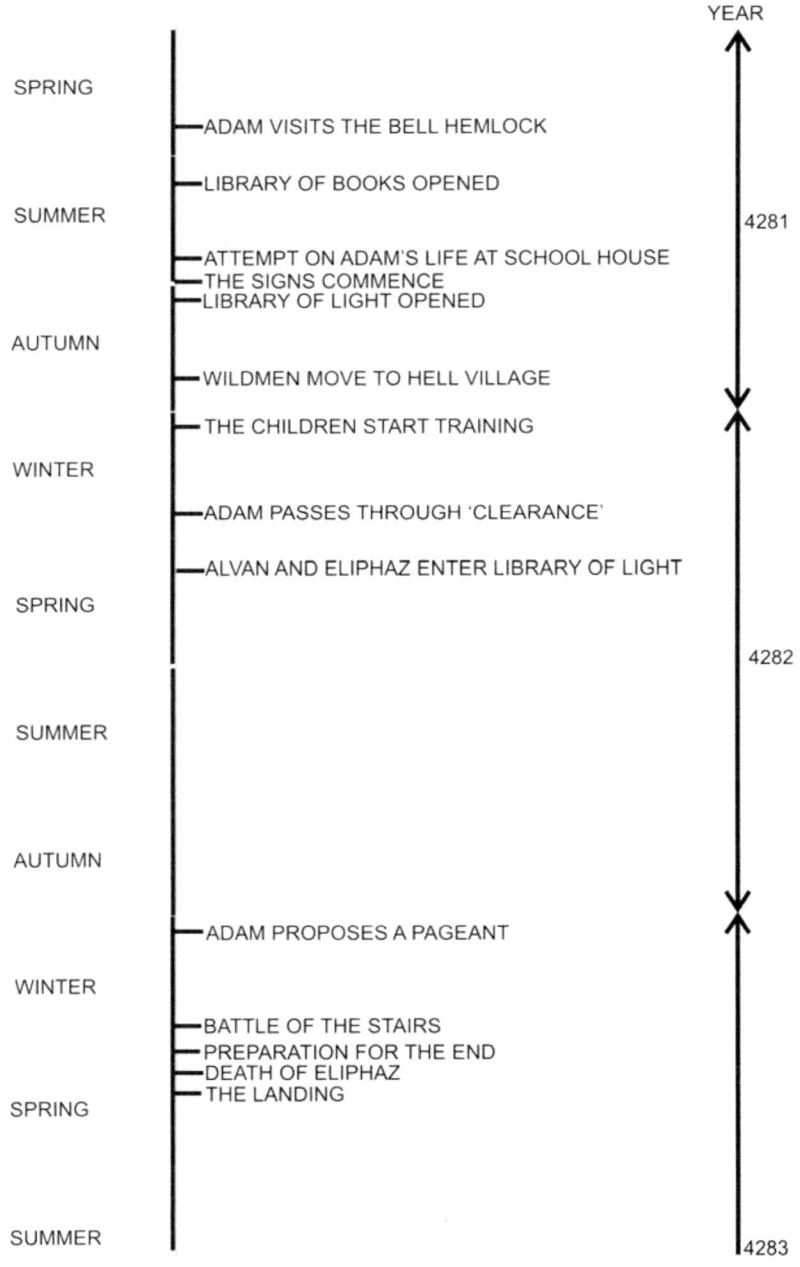

189